Coming
Together

Coming Together

DAVE JACKSON

Bethany Fellowship INC.
MINNEAPOLIS, MINNESOTA 55438

All scripture references are from the Revised Standard Version unless otherwise noted.

Copyright © 1978
Bethany Fellowship, Inc.
All rights reserved

Published by Bethany Fellowship, Inc.
6820 Auto Club Road, Minneapolis, Minnesota 55438

Printed in the United States of America

Library of Congress Cataloging in Publication Data

Jackson, Dave.
    Coming together.

    Includes index.
        1. Christian communities.   2. Christian communities—
United States.   I. Title.
BV4405.J32   301.34   78-16123
ISBN 0-87123-087-9

Table of Contents

Preface

It has been five years since Neta and I finished writing *Living Together in a World Falling Apart.* As a result of the travel and research we did for that book, we have remained at Reba Place Fellowship, the Christian community to which we moved after our four-year experience in a smaller one. Reba Place has just had its twentieth anniversary and has tripled in size in these last five years; there are now about 300 people involved with the community. Fourteen extended family households and dozens of nuclear family apartments are all located within walking distance in south Evanston.

Following a period of training and growth in one of those households, Neta and I were called to start a new household within the Fellowship. The Lord gave us the name "the Branch" from John 15. At one point the seams of the Branch's small group were bursting with 18 in-household people and three out-of-house members who lived in apartments nearby. After a couple of years the Branch divided and another household began, led by a couple who were trained in the Branch. Our household has now reduced in size to 12 people plus two nuclear families living in apartments outside. The smaller size was partially to help me work on this book and to allow more efficient ministry within the household. Neta is my first line editor as well as the household manager. We've both been enjoying the early years of our second child, Rachel Joy. Julian is almost nine now, full of community life and school, and a great delight.

Living Together has gone through many reprintings and has circulated far more broadly than we or the publisher expected. As a result we have received hundreds of letters from people all over the world telling about their efforts and experiences in Christian community. There seems to be no decline of interest in closer Christian fellowship. But while we have heard of many communities established, many others have failed—possibly as many as one-third of the attempts. In those that have collapsed there has often been great pain and hurt because people had risked the vulnerability of putting their lives on the line.

Certain communities fail while others succeed. Why? Though all situations are unique, three commitments are most critical: the willingness of the community to accept oversight, the quality of leadership, and the nature and depth of the members' commitment to the Lord. The risk is so great in starting a brand new community that we have a standard bit of advice: "Don't try to start your own! Go where it is already happening; submit yourself there and learn. Then later, if the Lord wants you to be part of starting a community, the idea can have adequate testing, support and oversight." Communities that are planted by other communities have the highest rate of survival.

This book is divided into three sections corresponding to the three crucial commitments for healthy community life. The news of the emerging networks describes the need we all have for oversight. And that section also offers ways we can better relate to the world. The section on internal organization speaks to the need for properly related and sensitively functioning leadership. The section on the personal implications of community suggests ways the individual can enter into a more transforming and radical Kingdom life.

Community life, as I speak of it in this book, is not restricted to the external characteristics of extended families or common purses. Such things are not the essence of community. They are merely tools.

(You can learn more about them in *Living Together*.) What I'm writing about in this book are churches or groups of Christians acting as the body of Christ. The distinguishing characteristic is a total commitment to discovering and doing God's will *in* the context of a local, self-conscious body of believers living with and under the authority of the Lord.

I draw heavily upon our experience at Reba and the other communities in our own network. However, the small group of communities with which I've been involved has been coming closer and closer to the other networks. We have been learning a great deal. For instance, much of the vision for what the Lord is doing to bring unity to His church is a vision broadly shared within the charismatic movement. It did not begin at Reba Place. Other subjects in the book are also not our private contributions and in some cases not even positions that we as a community have fully tested.

But there is such a similarity about what the Lord is doing—bringing His people together into active bodies, bringing those bodies into relationships of unity and brotherhood—that I get utterly exhilarated hearing about it. Many times I came across the same story: "The Lord's bringing us together, teaching us how to follow Him by living submissively in the church, and He's getting our church connected up with other churches."

One day, after talking to a visitor for only ten minutes, I jumped up and said, "Hallelujah! What confirmation! The Lord's been telling you the same thing He's been telling us." He was a part of a whole new network I'd never heard of before, and the Lord was teaching that group the same things I'd heard over and over again and bringing them together in the same way. When the Lord starts moving in that manner, He has a purpose; it's good news and worth telling.

Part One

Covenant Networks Emerge

1

Once, No People

Something has been happening in the church during the last five years. The charismatic movement has taken a turn toward a new objective. Those of us who have been renewed in the Spirit are finding that the Lord had more in mind than personal revitalization. He got our attention to ask us to do something. He wants us to come together.

The same is true for those of us who have been drawn into Christian communities. We are finding that the Lord brought us together for a larger purpose. He's asking our communities to reach out and link up with other communities, form networks, understand our identity, and become a people of God.

This uniting is an old theme in the church with a new urgency, an urgency that is brought by the Lord's call and confirmed by our circumstances. It is the formation of a self-conscious people distinct from the prevailing culture. It is not a new denomination but something that bridges the divisions between denominations, the organization of a Kingdom of people with a different allegiance, different basis, and different goals than those of secular society around it. It is a visible "underground," an alien people who are emerging from rather than dissolving into the melting pot.

For a long time Christians have believed that they were living in a Christian culture, tainted, of course, by sin and sinners who hadn't yet been transformed, but basically good. Their Christian vocation was to proclaim their faith and abstain from sin. But was there ever a Christian world culture? At best the world has been influenced and evil restrained by the church's presence acting as salt.

The biblical view of the Kingdom is consistently that of an alien culture within the world, never synonymous with the world. As the church recaptures the vision of being a distinctive people, our vocation becomes more than preaching and individual righteous living. We are hearing God's call to unite, to become one, to work at tearing down the barriers which separate all true believers.

To develop a sub-culture there must be interaction, and for there to be interaction there must be proximity. And that is happening too. Christians are choosing to live near each other, entering into relationships and commitments that allow God to forge a visible society. It's no longer enough to meet on Sunday morning in a beautiful sanctuary, sing some songs, and hear words of inspiration. It's no longer enough to have an annual crusade to convert the lost. If God is building a society, there must be responsibility for each other, accountability to each other, and a self-consciousness as a people. And that is happening.

This aspect of God's plan found new life with the development of Christian communities, and it is influencing the more traditional churches where members are establishing relationships with other members. Older Christians are discipling younger Christians, teaching them how to live in the Kingdom, helping them with their problems. Pastoral responsibility is being shared and focusing on the task of nurturing a flock of God's people.

But even more outstanding: during the last five years God has been leading these groups to reach out to one another. People who had learned the value of a deep commitment to each other within a community could envision the same kind of relationship between communities, and they began to draw together.

For instance, four years ago Reba Place Fellowship in Evanston, Illinois, entered into a formal covenant with three other communities: Plow Creek Fellowship in Tiskilwa, Illinois; Fellowship of Hope in Elkhart, Indiana; and New Creation Fellowship in Newton, Kansas. Our commitment to each other is unlimited and has, in fact, had the effect of making us feel like we are one body in four locations. We felt that there was value in formalizing our covenant, not that we could put on paper the totality of our commitment or that what we wrote would be restrictive, but we wanted to put into words at least the minimal elements. It is as follows:

> Over the past several years, the Lord has been leading us into a clearer and more explicit covenant among several Christian communities. The same kind of sharing which we find so significant within our communities, also has an application in the relationship between communities. We are grateful for this opportunity to be learning about this and putting it into practice. Some of the things which we hold in common are as follows:
> 1. A total commitment to Jesus is the basis for membership in each of the communities. This involves faith in Jesus as God's chosen Messiah. We believe that He has been raised from the dead and exalted as Lord. Our faith involves us in a personal relationship to Jesus growing out of repentance and giving everything to Him. From Him we receive forgiveness and the gift of the Holy Spirit.
> 2. Each of the communities has a style of life based upon the radical teachings of Jesus. This involves many changes in the way we live our lives, including, specifically, a renunciation of property rights and full sharing of all that we have; sacrificial love as an alternative to anger, violence, and war; faithfulness in marriage as the context for sex; a servanthood stance in all human relationship as so clearly revealed by Jesus; and communal organization of our personal lives as the setting in which we live out this discipleship.
> 3. Each community has the consciousness of being a local church, with all of the duties, privileges, and responsibilities of the body of Christ. This includes the authority to bind and loose in controversial ethical decisions, as Jesus suggested in Matthew 18.

Maintaining open and honest communication among all the members, with each one subject to the authority of the church, is an important aspect of this understanding.

4. *Each community seeks to carry out the Great Commission (Matt. 28 and Luke 24), both in its definition of world mission and in an openness to the Baptism of the Spirit in power, with all of its accompanying ministries, miracles, and growing pains.*

5. *Within the circle of these communities, we want to encourage and develop ways of helping each other:*

   —*encourage the sharing of spiritual gifts and resources through visits of leadership persons, letters, phone calls, and meetings for specific purposes.*

   —*respond seriously to any word of correction that may be brought to us by other groups or individuals.*

   —*be more free in personal visits between communities, exchange of people for work projects, and other similar activities which strengthen and enrich our common life.*

   —*be ready to transfer members from one group to another whenever this is the best way to serve the needs of some individual or meet the needs of a particular group. Such transfers need to be carried out with a clear leading from the Lord which is carefully tested in both communities.*

   —*be ready to share finances. Financial emergencies too large for one group could be met through pooling of resources from various groups. The initiation of unique projects or the funding of joint ministries would be other areas of cooperation.*

   —*schedule occasional gatherings of as many members as possible from all of the participating communities. These might continue to occur about once a year, although more frequent gatherings could be called as necessary. Leadership persons from the various communities would also continue meeting and consulting with each other as necessary.*

6. *As we affirm our relationship to each other within*

this circle of Christian communities, we also want to affirm our desire to be as open to other Christian groups as we are to these Christian groups. We are grateful for these relationships, but we know that this cluster is just one small fragment within the larger Christian movement. Recognizing what God has given us in this relationship and making the most of it should not prevent us from seeking the deepest possible relationship with other Christian groups and organizations. In fact, the positive nature of our relationship to one another within this circle should encourage us in developing other relationships.

7. *We welcome the participation of other Christian communities who wish to join with us. The process by which new communities are added will be similar to that by which individuals become members in each of our local communities [through a time of exploration and testing]. The specific procedures for this will evolve as we get more experience in relating to new communities.*

Since the formation of this network several other communities have explored the possibility of joining and are at various stages in that process. And we have adopted the name "Shalom Covenant" for our cluster.

The covenant has had a lot of practical testing despite its newness. The elders of all the communities get together at least four times a year to work on policy questions. We try to bring most of the members from all communities together for an annual conference. Each community receives an annual, week-long visitation from a team of one or two elders from each of the other communities. We have frequently had short or long-term exchanges of members. Money, at times in substantial amounts, has gone back and forth according to need.

Reba Place Fellowship also felt led to join the Old Mennonite and Church of the Brethren denominations. This was not to distinguish ourselves from other denominations but to affirm our relationship with some of the larger groupings in Christ's church by acknowledging our heritage. The members at Reba Place come from many denominations, but the community, born 20 years ago, was strongly influenced by the Anabaptist tradition of these churches. To join these denominations was to affirm the community's heritage and declare that we are part of the same body rather than separate from them, as our previous independence had implied.

For many of us it was a new way to look at denominations. They needn't be masters that separate local congregations but servants of the whole body of Christ that preserve certain traditions and emphases from which we all can benefit and draw. Paul urged the Corinthians not to allow his teachings or the teachings of Apollos or the teachings of Peter to be the occasions for division in the body, but to see them each as servants, each bringing something valuable to the whole body. We can enjoy the same ministry from the various denominations if we do not cut ourselves off from one another or imply that any grouping is the "one true church."

Shortly after our circle of communities reached out and joined one another, the same thing began to happen in another circle. More than two years ago about a dozen other communities began an exploratory courtship with each other. They are already-established communities which had been strongly influenced by Graham Pulkingham, earlier involved with the Church of the Redeemer Community in Houston, Texas. Known as the Community of Communities, they include the Fisherfolk Communities of Celebration in Colorado, England and Scotland; Sojourners in Washington, D.C.; Voice of Calvary in Mississippi; Christ's Church (Christian Reformed) in Grand Rapids, Michigan; the Church of the Messiah in Detroit; the Church of the Redeemer in Houston; and several other communities based in Episcopal parishes.

After a year this circle of communities established a "fellowship-based" commitment to one another. They did not choose to express that in a formal covenant, feeling that might restrict their commitment or tend to exclude others from participation. Instead, these communities wanted the intensity of their life together to grow out of their practical experience. They've now been together as a circle of communities over a year and are continuing to deepen their relationships.

In the meantime another type of network had been developing among the ecumenical communities, many of which began from Catholic charismatic prayer groups. The Word of God, a very large community in Ann Arbor, Michigan, and the People of Praise in South Bend, Indiana, realized that they were working together more and more closely in the publication of *New Covenant* magazine, Servant Publications, the administration of the Charismatic Renewal Service and other ministries. They were being called as a team to help establish and nurture new communities across the country and around the world. They and a number of other similar communities began developing closer ties. It was a response to the realization that just as individual Christians can get into trouble by themselves, so can communities.

The communities involved in this association include the Servants of the Light in Minneapolis, Minnesota; the Word of God in Ann Arbor, Michigan; the Work of Christ in Lansing, Michigan; the People of Praise in South Bend, Indiana; and the Lamb of God in Timonium, Maryland. These communities, in addition, are in contact with several other communities around the world, and some of these, in turn, will likely become part of the association of communities.

Two examples of the depth and seriousness of the relationships in this circle are demonstrated by the willingness of families to move across the country and entrust their whole lives to another community. John the Baptist community in San Francisco began hearing the Lord tell them in January 1977 that they all should move to South Bend, Indiana, and join the People of Praise. The reasons for moving could be summed up in the understanding that as the Lord was forming a people, the personal needs of the members of the John the Baptist community could be best met in South Bend, and the mission that God had for the People of Praise needed the help of those from San Francisco. Within six months all 150 members of John the Baptist community sold their homes, left their jobs and careers, and moved 2000 miles east, where God provided new homes and new jobs for each one of them.

A similar experience happened for an ecumenical community in Grand Forks, North Dakota. There, another 150 people moved to join the Servants of the Light in Minneapolis, Minnesota. In neither instance were the larger communities soliciting the moves. The initiatives came from the groups that moved as they listened and then tested leadings from the Lord.

The Shalom Covenant communities of which Reba Place is a part has entered into serious dialogues with both the ecumenical communities and the Fisherman Community of Communities about how the Lord may want us to deepen the relationships between our groupings. There are significant differences, particularly between the ecumenical communities and the Fisherman Community of Communities, but we want to be open to the growth of relationship.

On a local level the Lord is also building important relationships which tie together various networks of communities. Elders from five Chicago-area communities have been meeting regularly to forge a strong and trusting bond between us and listen to the Lord about what He might have for us to do in the Chicago area. Those communities are the Austin Community Fellowship, Daystar, Gospel Outreach, Jesus People USA, and Reba Place Fellowship.

Another style of communities that the Lord is building is the "ministry" networks. There are several of these networks of which Gospel Outreach is one example. They began in 1971 with about 30 young believers trying to make an old Coast Guard lighthouse station near Eureka, California, into a place of outreach with the gospel of Jesus Christ. Commonly known as the Lighthouse Ranch Ministry, these folks developed an evangelistic community life under the guidance and teaching of Jim Durkin, then a local pastor.

God led them into a pattern of growth and expansion of sending out new teams to begin communities in other cities as soon as they were able. Currently they have communities in 12 cities in the United States plus one in Guatemala and one in Germany. They average over 100 people each.

Recently their ministry has broadened, but initially they reached mostly young people, many of whom had been burned out on the road or through drug abuse. Each community shares a common purse and supports itself through the establishment of small businesses in which the members work very industriously. Some of their most successful enterprises have been vinyl and leather repair, cleaning services, and reforestation contracts.

The presiding elders from each of the cities gather periodically to help give direction for the ministry as a whole. Jim Durkin and others offer oversight and visit each community to keep a close sense of unity. The organic connection of being sent out and started by another community affords a strong relationship throughout the network.

Another, somewhat different witness to God's work of bringing His people together took place in 1974 with the Society of Brothers. The Society of Brothers began nearly 60 years ago in Germany as Eberhard Arnold began gathering a group of families and singles to live out the vision of church life that he saw in the New Testament. Chased from Germany by Hitler in 1937, they went first to England, and then in the middle of the war ventured across the Atlantic to settle in Paraguay until 1954 when some communities were started in the United States. By 1961 the whole Society had migrated north. There are now three of their communities in the United States, numbering about 350 each, and another that has been re-established in England.

They actually operate as one community with a private telephone line between each of the Bruderhofs (as they are called) in the States. By means of microphones and speakers they are able to have joint meetings between all three communities. However, the real miracle of unity for them was their re-unification with the Hutterite Church.

In 1931 Eberhard Arnold made a trip from Germany to the United States to visit the Hutterite church that had maintained a communal life for 400 years. (There are now about 25,000 Hutterites in North America.) He found that they essentially represented the New Testament vision that the Lord had given to him. He joined the church, himself being accepted as a Hutterite elder and established his community as a Hutterite colony. However, Eberhard died in 1935 from complications after an unsuccessful surgery on his leg. The unexpected loss of his leadership, pressure from the war, the years of migration, and much internal faithlessness deteriorated the life of the community seriously even though dedicated seekers continued to join.

In 1955 the unity that Eberhard had forged with the Hutterites came to a bitter end at Forest River, North Dakota. Several members of that Hutterite colony wanted to join the Society's community in Woodcrest, New York. In the ensuing conflict with the Hutterites, the Society took possession of the Forest River Colony for a time, forcing those members who were not in favor of that action to leave their own colony. In 1964 a serious attempt was made to repair the break with the Hutterians. However, most contacts were unprofitable and deepened the breach until the hostility and suspicion was quite pronounced on both sides.

Finally, however, as a result of the Spirit's urging, a deep repentance and spiritual renewal began taking place within the Society. Communitarian humanism that had eroded the life was cast aside, and hearts were turned toward Jesus. Heini Arnold, Eberhard's aging son, was able to realize a prayer that had been in his heart for years. With the full support of the community, he led four of the other leaders to a meeting with the ministers of the Hutterian church in Manitoba in January 1974. There, on behalf of the Society, he made a full confession and pled for forgiveness for the arrogant and sinful way that they had treated the Hutterians. Although he was the least personally guilty of those who represented the Society in Forest River, he offered to accept total responsibility for the errors on both sides. He was willing to accept whatever discipline the Hutterites might require of him.

Joe Maendel, a Hutterite who had been at Forest River in 1955, said, "Many of those ministers came to that meeting with stones of accusation in their pockets, ready to throw them. But when they heard what Heini had to say and the humility with which he said it, their hearts melted. There was nothing they could do but extend forgiveness and offer complete reconciliation and unification. It was completely of God."

I've often thought of that story and the courage and humility that Heini expressed. How many times will it have to be repeated as we dismantle the barriers that divide the church?

Another kind of unity is expressed by the relationships that exist between Derek Prince, Ern Baxter, Don Basham, Bob Mumford, and Charles Simpson. The network that they lead may represent the largest number of Christians who are personally allowing their everyday lives to be knit together with other Christians. The Bible teaching of these men has influenced believers around the world. One aspect of their teaching is that each Christian should be accountable to a pastor who will help shepherd them. Thousands who follow this teaching are submitted to leaders of small groups. These leaders are in turn accountable to someone else. And they are accountable to the men at the core of the network. The core group submits to each other as an avenue of submission to the Lord.

This creates a very workable network even though the strongest relationships are vertical—between each person and his "head." The Bible teaching is sound and life is dynamic. There is an increasing sense of peoplehood, and in some places there is the development of covenanted communities.

Even the 1977 Conference on Charismatic Renewal in the Christian Churches that took place in Kansas City is a genuine expression of God's hand in bringing His people together. Though the conference lasted only four days, the broad affirmation of the 50,000 participants underscored the theme of unity in Christ.

The conference statement speaks boldly of what the Lord is doing when it says, "We believe that this conference is a prophecy in action. We believe it is a prophetic statement in the church that in many ways unity is here now and that fuller unity is coming! We believe it is a statement to the nation and to the world that we who have been divided do love one another and that we will to be one so that the world may believe that Jesus is Lord."

That, in fact, gets to the core of what has been going on in the charismatic and community movements during the last few years. It alludes to John 17 which is Jesus' prayer for us. We pray for the things we want most. Jesus did the same, and because His prayer is recorded, there is no question about the Lord's highest will for our lives. He asked the Father to make us one, and He asked it again and again in that prayer. In Jesus' mind our unity is essential to fulfill His mission in the world. Whenever we resist that unity, we resist the Lord's will.

Of course there are many ways that we are not yet one. We must be ruthlessly honest in acknowledging the differences and barriers between us if the unity, when it comes, is to mean anything. But the goal of coming together is the Lord's will. It is His plan for the salvation of the world. For too long we have searched for some shortcut to evangelism. We thought we could develop a better plan for convincing the world that Jesus is the Christ. But He said that we will need to become "perfectly one, so that the world may know that thou [the Father] hast sent me and hast loved them even as thou hast loved me" (John 17:23). There's no other way. We must give ourselves to that molding by the Spirit.

Becoming as perfectly one as Jesus was with the Father involves far more than arriving at agreement about religious doctrine. Unity in our understanding of the truth *is* important because serious disagreements can create separation. In the same prayer Jesus asked that we'd be "sanctified" or purified in the truth. But much of our disunity is not over such serious disagreements that we could not get together if we each were willing to be molded by the Spirit of truth and if each of us made that preparation for unity our top priority.

But Jesus' unity is far more than unity on issues. It is relationship, commitment, throwing our lives together, becoming a people of God rather than persons for God.

Will we make ourselves available so God may answer Jesus' prayer, or will we cancel His order by insisting on our independence? In the last few years I have heard from hundreds of small groups of Christians who were wanting to begin community. However, many times they want advice rather than supervision and relationship from established communities. They want to do it *their* way in the place of *their* choosing. We have seen that attitude result in slow growth and frequent tragedies. The independent spirit of groups who insist on doing community on their own is sometimes only one step removed from the individualism that keeps other folks from trying community at all.

An affirmative response to Jesus' will that we come together has several levels of surrender and almost always involves giving up some of our independence: there is the giving of ourselves to relationships with other believers in commitments that cannot be dissolved. But there is also the giving of our group to other groups. That's a further surrender because more may be asked of us. We might be asked to give ourselves to many needy strangers. Or those with more experience may discern that our group doesn't really have what it takes to make it alone, and they may recommend that we all move and join with God's people elsewhere to learn and strengthen forces there.

But that kind of surrender is what it means to give

ourselves totally to the unity God is making of His Kingdom. As Peter said, "You are a chosen race, a royal priesthood, a holy nation, God's own people.... Once you were no people but now you are God's people; once you had not received mercy but now you have received mercy" (1 Pet. 2:9, 10).

2

The Prophetic Call

Why have the networks of communities begun to emerge, and why has the theme of unity in the body become prominent? "Surely the Lord God does nothing, without revealing his secret to his servants the prophets. The lion has roared; who will not fear? The Lord God has spoken; who can but prophesy?" wrote the ancient prophet Amos (Amos 3:7, 8).

Recently the lion of circumstances has roared again, and God has spoken to comfort us with His presence and prepare us for action. Jesus revealed an objective in His prayer for unity. It was basically an objective of evangelism: "That the world may know that thou hast sent me and hast loved them" (John 17:23). But the Lord seems to be revealing more about the circumstances of the time ahead of us.

The messages can be summed up in the words spoken at the 1975 International Charismatic Conference. "Because I love you, I want to show you what I am doing in the world today. I want to prepare you for what is to come. Days of darkness are coming on the world, days of tribulation. Buildings that are now standing will not be standing. Supports that are there for My people now will not be there. I want you to be prepared, My people, to know only Me and to cleave to Me and to have Me in a deeper way than ever before. I will lead you into the desert. I will strip you of everything that you are depending on now, so you depend just on Me. A time of darkness is coming on the world, but a time of glory is coming for My church, a time of glory is coming for My people. I will pour out on you all the gifts of My Spirit. I will prepare you for spiritual combat; I will prepare you for a time of evangelism that the world has never seen."

The Lord intends to use the strong relationships that are possible in community to help energize His church for the challenge. In the fall of 1976 at a conference at South Bend, Indiana, attended by more than 3,000 people living in Christian communities from around the world, this message came: "I am going to prune My church the way a man prunes a fruit tree to remove that which is dead and will never bear fruit. I will prune it by making it no longer easy for men to say, 'I will follow the Lord.' That which remains can then grow and bear greater fruit.

"I want you to have a great loyalty to one another and to Me because the time when I am going to prune My church is coming much sooner than you think. I want you to have this loyalty so that you can trust that you will not abandon one another under stress.

"And to you leaders in these communities, I say that you ought to be prepared for what I am going to require of you. To be a leader is to be asked to go first, and so I will teach you first, and I want you to learn thoroughly what it means to listen to My voice and obey. You will not be privileged among your brothers and sisters to meet a lesser standard. I will require the greatest faithfulness, truthfulness and integrity of you so that you will do whatever I tell you to do, and so that where I lead, you will go. Then you can say to My people, 'This is the way, follow in it.' "

This message calls us to link up and learn how to trust each other so that His church will not crumble and collapse when the time of shaking brings everything else tumbling to the ground. It is in preparation for a fulfillment of Hebrews 12:26-29 where it is written, " 'Yet once more I will shake not only the earth but also the heaven.' This phrase, 'Yet once more,' indicates the removal of what is shaken, as of what has been made [by men], in order that what cannot be shaken may remain. Therefore let us be grateful for receiving a kingdom that cannot be shaken, and thus let us offer to God acceptable worship, with reverence and awe; for our God is a consuming fire." The objective of the shaking is to reveal more clearly that which cannot be shaken—the Kingdom.

In some ways certain expressions of these challenges are already upon us. Within less than a year one of the communities which heard the prophecy at the 1975 International Charismatic Conference about buildings and supports no longer standing, returned to their home in Beirut, Lebanon, to find one of the most stable Middle East countries erupt in violence and chaos. For them buildings literally collapsed and the machinery of society ground to a halt. Certainly the persecution in Uganda and some of the South American countries can best be withstood by a deeply committed, tightly knit church. Of course the church has faced hard times before, even universal persecution, and the social structure has broken down in the Dark Ages and during world wars, famines and plagues. So what's the point of the prophecies? The point is our response and obedience.

We might speculate on what this means in terms of God's timetable for history. When Jesus was asked to give details of that timetable, He answered by describing signs and said that only the Father knew the exact day and hour, but we would be able to recognize the approaching season as surely as you can predict the coming of summer when the new, tender leaves appear on the fig tree. We can look at our circumstances and see that nuclear proliferation, fuel shortages, pollution, the possibility of terrorists using nuclear threats, and other conditions set us up for crises which are qualitatively beyond what could have ever been imagined in the past.

But that's not the point of the prophecies. They do not give a definitive statement on whether we are now facing "the end time." The emphasis is on *how* we should live. The only *why* revealed is that it is part of God's plan for bringing men and women to himself. It has always been right for the Christian to live expecting the imminent return of Christ. Our response should not be out of fear, but out of obedience to a loving Father who is looking out for His children by reviving for them the best way to live—come what may.

From the beginning the Lord has spoken to prepare His church for the circumstances it would face. In Acts 11 we can read how the Holy Spirit prompted some prophets to tell the people about a coming famine so that the believers in the Antioch church could prepare and send food for the relief of their brothers and sisters in Jerusalem. So it is not surprising when He does as much for us.

The kind of a commitment that the Lord is calling people to is not an easy one. It is especially demanding because part of its purpose is purification and toughening. Another of the prophecies shared at the communities' conference in South Bend explains the call.

"In order to be able to hear Me, you simply must be willing to give up everything. My plan cannot succeed through a mixture of your desires and My word to you. You must give up everything. I know what this means to you. For those of you who are young, it means laying down before Me the choices for your very life. For those who are older, it means laying before Me the entire life that you have built up over the years. And I want you to understand that this great cost that is exacted in order for you to be able to hear My word is to enable you to serve Me; it is not required for your personal salvation. If you do not wish to give up everything, then I ask you now as your loving Father, to withdraw from this people that I am drawing together. Your brothers and sisters will continue to love you. I will love you nonetheless. But I am at work to gather and to consolidate a people who are totally committed to My purpose. If you wish to stay with this people but come to find it difficult, your brothers and sisters will sustain you, and as you turn to Me, I will change your heart to allow you to move fully into the commitment that I ask.

"I want you to understand further that it is ultimately true that I, God Almighty, do not depend on any man to fulfill My plan. And yet because of the way that I have chosen to work in this age, it is a truth for the present that to accomplish My plan I am calling forth a people. It need not be a large people, but they must be totally dedicated to Me and totally committed to My word. However, in spite of that high cost they shall become a mighty multitude, and those who give up all for Me shall lead the richer life."

Men have wondered and even criticized the modern charismatic movement and the revival of Christian community because they could not see the purpose in it. "If all these gifts are truly from the Holy Spirit," they ask, "why has God chosen this time in history to revive what has had such little expression for so many centuries?" These prophecies suggest that God is pouring out His Spirit in a special way because His people need it in this modern era when we are all the more aliens. He has been drawing His people close to Him, teaching them how to listen to Him, and now He has something to say to them. God has always done that for His people. These prophecies are not the kind intended to frighten the sinner into repentance; they are intended to encourage and prepare the church because God loves it and has a purpose for it.

Ever since God called forth His people from Egypt, He has always used at least three ways of communicating. Nature declares the glory of God. His written word provides a standard. And God's contemporary word comes to man in his daily need.

The Lord gave the Hebrews the Law—a written revelation by which they could test everything. But He also gave them the pillar of fire, the cloud, the shekinah over the Ark of the Covenant and Moses for their daily guidance. Then He spoke through the prophets, the word for the moment. Later their messages were canonized into the recorded revelation. John tells us that Jesus was the personified word—God's word become flesh, such a complete expression as to be all we needed to top off our standard, so that when His life and the formation of His church was adequately recorded, we had a complete Bible. These prophecies do not add to the Bible in the sense of providing any divergent information about God's character or plan of redemption for man. Such an insight would need to be categorically rejected as the seeds of a heretical cult. The Bible is our complete standard against which all else is tested. But that very Bible tells us that we were not left alone to squeeze our life from a book. Our time is still stretched by Emmanuel (God with us). He lives by His Spirit in the church. God sent His Spirit to be *our* daily word, to guide us into all truth and to show us the things that are to come (John 16:13).

3

Church-Communities and the World

Are church-communities good retreats for escapists? Are they a way to evade the problems of today and the troubles of tomorrow? "Will you flee the world or heal it?" someone asked, anxious about the apocalyptic emphasis of some of the prophecies, the close-knit and disciplined life of the communities and the report that some groups had pulled up stakes and moved across the country.

But were those moves a frightened run for the hills? Or were they a consolidation in obedience to God's call and direction? Most of the major moves that I am familiar with—the move of the John the Baptist community from San Francisco to Indiana, the unification of groups into the Servants of the Light community in Minneapolis, the move of about 50 people from Houston to Denver to form the Beyond Jordan community, the move of Sojourners from Chicago to Washington, D.C., the consolidation of some smaller communities at Reba Place Fellowship—were direct responses to leadings that each group sincerely believed were from the Lord. The people were not attempting to escape the world's problems, and they would have remained where they were, no matter what the conditions were, if that had been God's direction.

Among the communities where the prophecies of hard-times-to-come have had the most airing, there has not been a flood of people coming because of those messages. Paul DeCelles of the People of Praise said that the prophecies have had very little influence on *why* people have come to that community. "If anything, more people have left as a result of the prophecies. We expect that communities may be used by the Lord as bulwarks to absorb and thwart the hardest blows of evil in the land. Some people realized that they could not make a commitment to that kind of sacrifice."

Yet we are encouraging *all* Christians to become part of a solid, community-type body, not necessarily one with households and a common purse (as useful as those are), but a church with fully coordinated and submitted members who will stand as one. And we are hearing the Lord call those communities to grow and create trusting relationships between each other. The testimony of that kind of unity within the body of Christ may be the most important role of service that the church has to offer to the world in these days. Every Lone Ranger evangelist, missionary, healer, social reformer, prophet, peacemaker or teacher who has had an effective ministry can only improve that ministry by submitting it to the supervision of the body in which the Lord intends it to be based. If we are truly interested in serving the world, I believe that we must begin from a church base. That is not a withdrawal. It is a call for integrity and strength.

Given the solid base of being at one in the Lord, there are several motifs in the Bible depicting the roles in which God's people can serve the world. To name just a few: we are to be suffering servants, the light of the world, a city on a hill, a city of refuge, salt, and the intercessors for the world.

The Voice of Calvary in Jackson and Mendenhall, Mississippi, offers a good example of how a community can be a suffering servant to the world. Started by John and Vera Mae Perkins in 1960, the community serves the poor blacks in the neighborhood by buying up old deteriorating houses to be renovated and sold or rented, and by operating a medical clinic, a gymnasium, a library, a cafeteria, a thrift store, and a new youth center. To entwine our lives with the poor, to accept their lot as our own, to absorb the oppression that bows the weak, and to stand condemned with the prisoner will always be part of the Christian's vocation. "He was despised and rejected by men, . . . Surely he has borne our griefs and carried our sorrows, . . . and with his stripes we are healed" (Isa. 53:3-5). "For to this you have been called, because Christ also suffered for you, leaving you an example, that you should follow in his steps" (1 Pet. 2:21). "The Spirit of the Lord is upon me, because he has anointed me to preach good news to the poor. He has sent me to proclaim release to the captives and recovering of sight to the blind, to set at liberty those who are oppressed, to proclaim the acceptable year of the Lord" (Luke 4:18, 19).

Bethany Fellowship in Minneapolis, Minnesota, exemplifies our calling as a light to the world. The evangelistic thrust of Bethany Fellowship Missions began in 1943 when a newly organized congregation of just 16 members received a missionary challenge to train, send and support 100 foreign missionaries. Now 490 people are involved with the Fellowship. The goal of 100 missionaries has been reached and almost doubled, and there is no plan to stop. The Lord has accomplished that remarkable work through them because they were willing to sell all of their possessions, pool their resources and work full time in the training center, publishing division or industry which manufactures camping trailers, electrical appliances and other electronic equipment that compete with the finest products in their field. Jesus said, "You are the light of the world. A city set on a hill cannot be hid. Nor do men light a lamp and put it under a bushel, but on a stand, and it gives light to all in the house. Let your light so shine before men, that they may see your good works and give glory to your Father who is in heaven" (Matt. 5:14-16).

That same text says that "a city set on a hill cannot be hid" and implies that potent evangelistic thrust comes through our very existence when it is a visible witness to the Kingdom. The Society of Brothers does this in a very inspiring way. They feel strongly about being in a rural setting where their communities can be largely self-contained with their own schools and their own industry, allowing members to live and work together where all things are done with the Kingdom in mind. Even though situated in a rural setting, their three communities in the United States and one in England are accessible to thousands of seekers each year, who get a small glimpse of the total life involvement that the Kingdom can inspire.

A different, but equally dramatic, "city on a hill" occurs when a community develops within a city. The Church of the Messiah in Detroit, Michigan, offers such a contrast. Located along Grand Boulevard, the community is in a very depressed neighborhood. There are worse slums, but few that feel so hopeless and disintegrated. Almost all sense of community has left the neighborhood as what were once near mansions have either crumbled to rubble or have been converted into ill-kept half-way houses, transcient rooming houses, cheap retirement homes, and poorly funded treatment centers for alcoholics, drug addicts and prostitutes. There are no business interests and few permanent residential interests to give the neighborhood cohesiveness. No one seems to care—except for the Church of the Messiah. Its actual church building is a hub of daily service and interest. The households can be picked out by walking down the street and noticing their warm, cared-for appearance. The people greet one with a twinkle in their eye, not a hopeless stare. Their day care center is filled with color, and their grade school is the only safe one in the neighborhood. Their light gives hope and light to all in their neighborhood and it gives glory to the Father.

Almost all of the communities are fulfilling the role of a city of refuge. Reba Place Fellowship is just one example. All of the members have come with needs that were not being met as they lived alone. Some arrived in a very broken state, truly in need of a refuge. There is a real sense in which contemporary life with its sin, pollution, competition, tension and breakdown of social support structures is not healthy for human beings. There is a legitimate role for communities to fulfill in inviting people in out of the storm. Jesus said,

"Come to me, all who labor and are heavy laden, and I will give you rest" (Matt. 11:28). Reba Place is glad to do that for all who will come, even though the community can't change the conditions for all of those who won't come. Whether it was Noah and his ark or the serpent on the pole in the wilderness or the actual cities of refuge in the Land of Canaan, God has offered salvation to those who would receive it.

The Sojourners community in Washington, D.C., is a good example of a community that is performing the function of salt. In 2 Thessalonians 2:3-7, Paul indicates that the full force of evil in the world is currently being restrained, presumably by the Holy Spirit who indwells the church. It may be for this reason that Jesus said, "You are the salt of the earth" (Matt. 5:13). Throughout the centuries corrupted religion has often added to the problems of the world, but nonetheless the church has, in its faithful times and ways, profoundly affected civilization for the good. The Sojourners community has located itself in Washington, D.C., for the purpose of living out a prophetic witness in the heart of the country's government. The members of the community actively speak out on issues of government policy in such areas as foreign aid to countries which torture prisoners, defense spending, peace, housing for the poor, corruption and many other issues. In some quarters, they have gained a hearing. One perspective they bring to those dialogues is the view that the church should not be the expression of a civil religion which allows its morals to be molded by the necessities and pressures of the immediate situation. When the church slips into civil religion, its function becomes the justification of the policies of the government. The Sojourners want to avoid that role toward any political system. Rather they want to hold the Gospel up as the standard against which all things are measured.

Monastic communities have long accepted the responsibility of prayer and intercession for the needs of the world and the church. It is a worthy task. Even in the story of the cities of Sodom and Gomorrah we can see that God was willing to extend His tolerance and forestall His judgment many times simply because of the earnest prayer of Abraham. The Jesus Brotherhood in Germany is one community which takes seriously its responsibility to pray for the needs of the church and the world. Though they have many other forms of ministry, they corporately stop their work five or six times a day for prayer. One of those times is devoted to intercession for the unity of the body of Christ and at another time they pray more broadly for the needs of the world. That's not so glamorous as some deeds might seem, but its value may rank above any.

There are several other biblical motifs for the roles that the church should fulfill in the world as it represents Christ. We must constantly be learning how to be concerned about the needy people of the world; our doors must be open and constantly receiving them in one way or another. However, we should never slip into the trap of trying to justify ourselves by our good deeds. It is humbling to realize that the actual dent we make on the overwhelming needs of the world is insignificant, certainly not a basis for our self-justification. But that's not why any of us should be following Jesus. We'll always fall short, and the good we can do in any arena offers little hope for the salvation of the world.

Our ministry to others is not because we think we can heal the world by *our* efforts; it must only be because God has asked us to love others and because sharing His love and compassion is consistent with the character of the Kingdom. This attitude of living in the Kingdom *now* is what is giving rise to a visible, Christian counter culture in the form of Christian communities. Their very existence is issuing a fairly strong indictment of the secular world's system. And that indictment becomes more poignant as we look at Scripture and confirming prophecies which suggest that the world's system will collapse.

It is tempting to recoil from that indictment and invest ourselves in the preservation and improvement of this world's system with the hope that one day it will evolve into the Kingdom of God. That's been the only hope for the coming of the Kingdom that many Christians have known.

However, I think there is a greater antithesis between this world's system and the Kingdom of God. This world's system can be seen as the product of man's rebellion, a rebellion from which each person must repent as he admits that his highest achievements are insufficient to save himself. The Kingdom of God is then an alternative rooted in the church rather than a refinement of this world's system.

The development of Christian communities is more in line with this view. Just as man's personal rebellion in stepping outside of God's Kingdom produced a fallen society, so must personal salvation result in man's re-entry, through the blood of Jesus, into a society where the very structures as well as the individuals recognize Jesus as Lord.

Like Jesus, who wept over Jerusalem, we anguish over the pain of the people suffering under the systems around us. We try to effect change, bring justice and ease hardship whenever possible because those deeds are consistent with the Kingdom, and we are to "live as in the day." But we do not pin our hopes for the fulfillment of the Kingdom on such isolated efforts. Ultimately this world's systems are under judgment because they are often the products of man's rebellion and easily become the tools of the "principalities and powers, the world rulers of this present darkness, the spiritual hosts of wickedness in heavenly places" (Eph. 6:12). The "healing of the nations" cannot come by anything short of repentance.

"We know that the whole creation has been groaning in travail together until now; and not only the creation, but we ourselves, who have the first fruits of the Spirit, groan inwardly as we wait" (Rom. 8:22, 23). God is "not wishing that any should perish, but that all should reach repentance. The day of the Lord will come like a thief, . . . and the earth and the works that are upon it will be burned up" (2 Pet. 3:9, 10).

Jesus' prayer in John 17 instructs us in the way we are to live until He returns to fulfill the Kingdom. Jesus said that we "are not of the world, even as I am not of the world. I do not pray that thou [Father] shouldst take them out of the world, but that thou shouldst keep them from the evil one.... I pray that they may be one even as we are one, I in them and thou in me, that they may become perfectly one, so that the world may know that thou hast sent me and hast loved them even as thou hast loved me." That commission is to come together in the world, not be separated and not withdraw.

The early Christians had a vivid image of our place in the world. Peter spoke of us as "aliens and exiles" who are to maintain our good conduct while we are in the world. (See 1 Pet. 2:11, 12.) Paul reminded the Philippians that even though they lived on earth, their commonwealth or citizenship was in heaven, and they should live accordingly. (See Phil. 3:20.) This analogy had special significance for the residents of Philippi which was a Roman colony because they knew the purpose of the colony.

Rome had established such cities all over the empire. They were colonized by Roman citizens, frequently retired military men and their households. They would structure their corporate life on the Roman pattern, build new buildings following the latest Roman architecture, introduce theatre and build amphitheatres, dress in Roman fashion, live by Roman law and exercise Roman culture in every way. The purpose was to provide the surrounding province with as complete an example of Roman society as possible with the expectation that people would be so impressed that they would want to become Roman citizens.

The City of Corinth was another prime example of this method of Romanization. In 46 B.C. Julius Caesar rebuilt the previously destroyed city and colonized it with his veterans. It soon became one of the five great cities of the Mediterranean world.

So, the early Christians understood the idea of being an alien people, a colony established in the world to spread a way of life by functioning as a visible expression of the Kingdom. They knew that they would be ineffective and subject to assimilation if they drifted off to live independently. Everywhere they went, everywhere they were driven, they would group together to form a body. That was their base for relating to the world.

Can similar groupings of Christians have any significance for the world today? I believe so. Living in community has many benefits and joys. The life is rich no matter how materially lean we run, but our influence in the world is very modest. Our only justification for "living in the day," for living as though the Kingdom has come will be Christ's return in glory and power. He alone will be able to extend what we have tasted to bring healing to all of creation.

"You must understand," Peter wrote, "that in the last days some people will . . . make fun of you and will ask, 'He promised to come, didn't he? Where is he? Our fathers have already died, but everything is still the same as it was since the creation of the world!

"But do not forget one thing, my dear friends! There is no difference in the Lord's sight between one day and a thousand years; to him the two are the same. . . . But the Day of the Lord will come. . . . What kind of people should you be? Your lives should be holy and dedicated to God, as you wait for the Day of God and do your best to make it come soon. . . . Look on the Lord's patience as the opportunity he is giving you to be saved" (2 Pet. 3:3-15, TEV).

4

Various Congregations /
Various Ministries

Paul was an efficient teacher; he could teach two truths in one lesson. Unfortunately, we are sometimes not so adept at learning. In Paul's teaching on relationships within the church in 1 Corinthians 12, he makes it clear that the body of Christ has many members with different gifts essential for different purposes. Therefore, no one needs to think of himself as inferior or superior. Everyone has a place; everyone is essential.

The double lesson is that these truths apply equally within a local congregation and between congregations in the church at large. If it is not already known before a community begins, this truth is quickly learned or the local church falls apart. We can neither be envying nor belittling one another and still stay in unity.

However, possibly because of geographic separation, we are not so aware of the damage created when we have this attitude between communities. It is easy to feel that because one community is so into evangelism, it must not have a sound body life or adequate discipleship care. Or because another is into inner healing, it is too introspective. Or because another is into prophetic witness or social services, it isn't spiritual enough. Or that another which lacks a witness to the simple life must therefore be too materialistic.

Obviously, a community may not have a sound body life and discipleship care, or another may be too introspective, or another might not be spiritual, or another may be materialistic. But those judgments don't necessarily follow the surface differences on which we often make them. And they don't take into account that the Lord may have ordained some of our differences precisely because we have different roles to fulfill in the church at large.

Our difficulty in accepting these differences in the body often stems from our own insecurity. Paul speaks to two responses of insecurity. The first is the comment of the "foot" which says, "Because I am not a hand, I do not belong to the body." This is usually an inferiority or jealousy struggle on the part of an individual who is always wanting to be someone else. It is not often the attitude of a whole church. Though some within a church are always wishing their church were different, the group as a whole usually generates plenty of justification for its existence.

The second common tendency is that of the "eye" or the "head" which says to the "hands" or the "feet," "I have no need of you." This opinion more often happens between congregations.

There may be some significance to the fact that in Paul's analogy he suggested that feelings of inferiority easily accompanied the feet, while feelings of superiority were ascribed to the eye and the head. That is so like us to think that service is unimportant while vision and direction have it all. If we've got the broad vision, it is so easy to look down on the community that is struggling with the mundane.

Actually, within the networks of communities the greatest tensions exist between the different types of communities. The overt ministries are not so frequently a barrier as are the internal structures and self-understandings. For instance, the Fisherman Community of Communities is primarily committed to the renewal of existing churches, often Episcopal parishes. This has led those communities to develop some very unique characteristics. Most of the communities reside within large parishes. There is a core group of people who participate in the community life, and there is often a much larger group of people that are simply members of the church. (This style is not true of the Communities of Celebration, which are set aside to support ministry teams. But the objective of the teams is to renew parishes and start the above-type communities within them.)

In their parish settings these communities do not clearly define memberships. If someone is a member of the parish church, how can there be another membership list in the context of the same congregation without creating two classes of Christians? Their solution is that their communities are "fellowship based." By this they mean that whoever participates is part of the community. This creates easy access to and regress from community living. These communities distinguish themselves from "covenant based" communities which have clear memberships and clear procedures for joining. They feel their style is open, non-judgmental and resists authoritarianism. They also feel that existing churches are unthreatened by their style because they remain within the church and don't cross denominational lines.

A different structure exists for the ecumenical communities such as the Word of God, People of Praise, or the Servants of the Light. They draw people from all denominations without requiring them to leave their home churches. They do this by not replacing the churches. They don't set up Sunday morning services or perform the sacramental duties of the various churches in any given town. They exist along side the other churches. Because participation in the communities does not imply two classes of Christians as it might if they were within a parish, they can be very clear about membership. These communities also have the advantage of experiencing the kind of unity in the body of Christ between denominations which many of us envision for the whole church. They are pioneering a brotherhood among believers that we all long to enjoy. Their ecumenical base also gives them an advantage in evangelism. They can invite people to come to Jesus without the inference that they are proselytizing for their own denomination.

The ecumenical communities are covenant based. This gives them the possibility of clearly explaining to any new people how they might go about exploring membership in the community. An explicit covenant gives the new person some insight into the extensive nature of the commitment, even though no written covenant can cover everything.

Clarity on membership benefits the visitor who is granted a place of free observation and learning until he is ready to submit himself and shoulder the responsibilities of membership. Anyone can sometimes have struggles with feelings of rejection. These covenant communities feel that they can diminish this problem by their clarity on membership. The outsider holds the key to entrance into membership, and the community can be freer from the charge of cliquishness or exclusiveness because membership, and thereby the feeling of acceptance, is not based on the intensity of interaction at any given moment.

One other aspect of the covenant-based communities is that there is clarity on the discipleship stance among the members. Those who are not members may seek the advice and counsel of the community, but there is an understanding that their trust level is not to the point of receiving firmer direction—they have not declared their accountability to the community. Members, however, have declared their accountability and have invited the community's authority to be operative in their lives. This leads to a freedom in sharing brotherly admonition and thereby enhances personal growth among the members.

A third prominent style among communities is the church-community where the two aspects, both the community and the church, are synonymous. Reba Place Fellowship is such a community. The community is not a sub-group within a local church, and it does not exist beside the church. It is the church, carrying with it all the rights, privileges and authority of a local church body. The members share the eucharist together; that is the context in which marriages and baptisms happen, and for the members the church-community is their center of gravity for spiritual authority.

Church-communities usually have a number of people who worship with them and participate in other degrees as non-members. But the community is not responsible for a large parish of quasi-committed members who would be offended if there were another membership within it. Thus, they also avoid two classes of membership. They uphold total commitment as the only basis for membership in the body. That may seem demanding, but they feel it is consistent with many of Jesus' teachings where He says things like, "Whoever of you does not renounce all that he has cannot be my disciple" (Luke 14:33).

Church-communities are also covenant based. They find no problems with being explicit about membership and the requirements for membership. Evangelism beckons the total person to leave all and follow Jesus as a whole new way of life. Compromised levels of commitment are not encouraged. The result is that the body as a whole demonstrates many of the ideal characteristics of the Kingdom.

However, for each of these styles of community there are some disadvantages—disadvantages that are sometimes met in the other style. The ecumenical communities struggle because they are not formally a church, but they are performing some of the most essential and neglected tasks of the church. The church-communities miss the opportunity to minister and fellowship with all the committed Christians in a town because some of those Christians cannot leave the other churches they are in. The parish-based communities lack the advantages of having clear commitments among the membership. And there are many other comparisons that could be cited. In each situation the advantages of one style ministers to people who couldn't be reached by the other style.

It is so easy for us to note the disadvantages of another style without seeing just how God is using that other part of the body to do a task we couldn't do. In the early church these same kinds of differences existed, and folks struggled with them in the same way. There was always the tendency to allow those differences to create tension and division. In the New Testament the greatest area of tension existed between the

Jews and Gentiles. The Hebrew Christians thought that the church should be set up in one way (and they had good reasons), and the Gentile Christians thought it should take another form (for equally valid reasons). If, as the leaders met and discussed these differences, they would have decided to follow one pattern or the other, the advance of the Kingdom would have suffered and some people would have not come to the Lord. Fortunately, the decision of the Jerusalem council was to affirm both styles as equally appropriate for their respective situations. Paul specifically uses the analogy of the body to appeal for an affirmation of brotherhood between the Jewish and Gentile Christians. All believers are members of the same body.

In one of the early meetings of elders from the communities that later joined to become the Fisherman Community of Communities, Graham Pulkingham made an important observation on the degree of similarity that needs to exist in order to experience "unity." Most of the communities in that network are centered in parish churches. But then there are the Communities of Celebration and such divergent fellowships as Sojourners with its magazine and prophetic witness and Voice of Calvary, a poor, mostly black community in rural Mississippi. Graham said that they didn't all need to be alike, but no community in the circle should be committed to something major that the others weren't also committed to. They all needed to be committed to it even if they weren't all doing it. What he meant was that Post Green Community in England didn't need to be identical to Voice of Calvary, but neither community should be doing anything that the other couldn't support.

That's how the early churches resolved the differences between them. They didn't homogenize or agree to follow only one style, but affirmed the rightness of both styles. As Paul reports, "James and Peter and John . . . gave me and Barnabas the right hand of fellowship, that we should go to the Gentiles and they to the circumcised" (Gal. 2:9). The Jerusalem church was committing itself to the way Paul was conducting his ministry even though those in Jerusalem were doing things differently.

That is what is meant by unity. Unity does not mean uniformity. Uniformity runs counter to the doctrine of various ministries and structures which is taught by the imagery of the body of Christ.

There are, of course, things that cannot be grafted into the body. Recent medical attempts at transplants show that a human body may reject certain organs, not because the body has no need of a new kidney, for instance, but because the kidney is sometimes of a very different type. The same is true of the body of Christ. The council at Jerusalem might have told Paul that they could not accept his ministry, in which case there could not have been unity without his change. The same may be true today. There may still be areas of difference that are so serious that unity cannot happen without some change. But we should do everything to test that before tolerating separation or insisting on uniformity in a particular area.

In response to the will of our Lord as revealed in His prayer, and in line with the moving of the Spirit today, the burden of proof is on those who would resist unity and relationship. There's already a mandate to unite so that any church or community which resists has to provide the overriding reason for not following Christ's wish.

Derek Prince, writing in *New Wine* magazine, said that he believes that God's next move is not going to be upon individuals, but upon bodies. He takes that from Ezekiel 37, the vision of the valley of dry bones, and he believes that that vision has another application for today. In the vision there were two moves by God. God told Ezekiel to first prophesy to the bones. Then He told him to prophesy to the winds.

Prophesying to the bones accomplished the re-assembly of the individual bodies. Prophesying to the winds gave those bodies life and power, stood them on their feet and assembled them into an exceedingly great army.

That's God's objective for today: an exceedingly great army!

5

The Peaceful Army

In 1968, more than a year before Neta and I became involved in Christian community, we were members of a black, storefront church on Chicago's West Side. The Lord had placed us there to learn many lessons. One of the lessons had to do with violence and power and has some implications for the future ethics of Christian communities. If God is calling His people to be a bulwark against the tide of evil, what kind of force will we use as we grow in strength? Or, to what force will we appeal if we are persecuted?

My lesson on the West Side had to do with a conflict of interests and methods between two systems. I was trying to be both a representative of God's Kingdom and a servant of this world's system as a member of the Illinois National Guard.

It was early spring.

I stood up in the army truck and watched the jeep at the front of the convoy turn left onto Roosevelt Road. In a few blocks we would be in the vicinity of my church.

With all the other parts of Chicago that were in flames following the assassination of Dr. Martin Luther King, Jr., why did our unit have to patrol this area? Our unit was usually stationed 30 miles outside the city. What would the kids think when they looked past a jagged bayonet and saw my white face? The last time they'd looked, I'd been their Sunday school teacher!

"Keep those weapons high!" the sergeant had

shouted. "Make those people see you mean business."

What kind of business *did* I mean? I remembered my basic training, the rifle range, and the shape of the targets. What in the world was I doing here?

There. Through the smoke. The tall guy in purple. Wasn't he the one who stood in the back of the church a couple of Sundays ago?

"We've come this far by faith, leaning on the Lord. . ." I could imagine Mrs. Wilkerson's black face singing in the choir. She lived in the apartment on the corner.

"Oh God," I prayed. "Don't let me make a mistake out here."

The truck jolted over the spider web of fire hoses in the street. I tugged my steel helmet low over my eyes and caught the glint of the ammunition strapped across my shoulder. Those live rounds sure had sharp points.

"Good shootin', soldier. You got the highest score in the company today."

"Thank you, sir."

That had been years before in training at Fort Ord. I looked down at my rifle and touched the front sights. They were loose and slid back and forth in the little groove. Were innocent people "safe" from my weapon?

"Where are the black troops?" shouted an angry old man on the sidewalk. "There ain't a soul brother among you. I don't care why you're coming down here; we don't want to be overrun by no white army."

The time dragged on until our "white army" had toured those blocks for a week. I didn't have to shoot or stab anyone. In fact, the only shooting I observed was done by the police. As for the National Guard, the guys yelled a lot of insults, calling people "niggers" and offering to "gang bang" the women, etc. A few of the citizens got pushed around and shaken up pretty badly. One night my lieutenant, thinking a sniper was hiding in a dark alley, led a few men in to locate the noise. He said he almost pulled the trigger before he realized it was just a child peeking out of his bedroom window.

But finally we gathered our dirty uniforms, rolled up our sleeping bags, and left.

Within a few months I was again armed and back on the streets of Chicago. This time it was a different part of the city—in front of the Conrad Hilton for the Democratic National Convention—but I again faced people that I knew. I had not expected to have to do that when I took the oath to obey orders upon joining the army.

At first I had enjoyed the army. Training presented challenges that I rose to rapidly. I even received a special citation from our colonel as the "Outstanding Trainee of the Cycle." I wouldn't let any amount of harassment or rough stuff get me down, and firing tracers from a 50-caliber machine gun at a rusted-out car body a half mile down range was more fun than skipping rocks across a pond. I was in the infantry, and most of my buddies were going to Vietnam, so we got trained on every kind of ingenious weapon.

But most targets were silhouettes of men. Sometimes that and the requirement to scream "Kill! Kill! Kill!" as we worked out with bayonets or hand-to-hand combat bothered me. But usually I just accepted the fact that we were defending our loved ones and our freedom from the "gooks." They were evil, far away, and deserving of death. I could do it.

Some of our instructors were a few of the first combat troops to return from Vietnam. They were some of the toughest, meanest men I'd ever met, but they had survived those early months of U.S. intervention. Two were still shell shocked—jumping and flinching at almost every abnormal noise. Those men told us of some of the same things Lt. Calley reported: An old woman might be carrying a gun; a six-year-old kid can walk up smiling and throw a hand grenade at you; everyone's the enemy; you're safe nowhere.

Some of the men had been on an interrogation team together. They proudly told of methods they had used to get information: beatings, near suffocation with urine-soaked rags, items pushed under fingernails, electric shocks to the genitals of both men and women, and if none of those things worked, you could always take three prisoners up in a helicopter and push the first two out—the third one was sure to tell you all you wanted to know.

One of my buddies timidly asked if all that wasn't against the internationally agreed upon laws of war we'd heard about in some of our earlier classes.

"Well, the VC do it to our men," the instructor barked. "Besides, when you've got someone in front of you who knows information that can save the lives of you and your men, just when are you going to stop trying to get it?"

Such is ultimately the way of war no matter how we'd like to dress it up. If the stakes are high enough, and if a person can remove the enemy far enough from him so that he is just a gook or a nigger or silhouette or coordinate on a map, he can do whatever is needed if he has once made a league with the Spirit of Violence as his source of protection. That spirit is a hard one to exorcise in the middle of a crisis because of his enormous powers of rationalization.

But I had not gone to a foreign combat zone or even a strange part of the city where I could distance myself from the "enemy" with the rhetoric of hate. They were real people with loves and lives and homes and children. I knew them and they were no enemy of mine. It haunted me that I had come to them with a gun and a bayonet and the threat of death; did I dare return in the name of the Lord and speak of His love?

Couldn't God have let me go across the ocean to brandish my weapons, or at least couldn't He have sent me to some strange neighborhood where I wouldn't have known anyone? Yes; I suppose He could have. But maybe He knew that I would have to have my nose pushed into the contradiction before I'd face the question.

"Is it right to kill?"

Reba Place Fellowship and each of the communities that we are in covenant with have felt that peace is a very critical area of discipleship for the church. A peace witness is first of all faithful to the clear teachings of Jesus and the practice of the early church, and that's most important. But there are other implications that are broadly related to how we view the church and its mission. Are we a peculiar and holy people that God is calling forth to build into His Kingdom which will someday supplant this world's system? Or is the church just a reforming force in this world's system intended to help society become better and better? If we are the former, then living as aliens who follow Kingdom standards regardless of their success in this system is faithfulness to our King. If our view is the latter, then there is a rationale for compromising the teachings of Jesus because society hasn't improved enough for them to be operative. One just does the best thing that will work. He might not enjoy war, but if it proves necessary, he can go along with it until it becomes unnecessary.

We see God's Word teaching that we are to be in the world but not of the world's system, and we do not feel history indicates any basic improvement in this world's system. So "let us conduct ourselves becomingly as in the day of the Lord's return" (Rom. 13:13). We want to live by those standards now as though Jesus has already returned with power and glory, because for us He has/will.

Even now there are practical applications. There's a good chance that the draft will be reinstituted in the future, and we must regularly consider how freely we pay our war taxes or support officials who do not work for peace. But there is a deeper concern: As the networks of communities and Christian groups have come together, there have been times when part of the movement has had a military tone. It has spoken of the Army of the Lord against the Forces of Evil. It has referred to the practice of submission and authority as being like captains, lieutenants and soldiers under our Commander-in-Chief, Jesus Christ. And it has sung rousing songs of a martial nature.

At first I was really shocked by all of that sword rattling because my experience had caused me to choose to serve God rather than man by getting a discharge from the military as a conscientious objector. But here I was running into communities which had taken no stand against military participation by their members, and furthermore they were talking about "going to war" themselves. I really wondered what side they'd end up on if there were no distinctions between the Army of the Lord and worldly military force.

However, it is a fact that we are in a battle, and things may very well get hot and heavy in times to come. So the question is not whether we are at war with evil, but how do we avoid treason? To have our consciousness raised part way (to realize that we are at war) leaves us particularly vulnerable to one of Satan's most subtle subversions—pursue the right ends by the wrong means. It is a powerful trick, maybe Satan's most powerful since he chose to try it on Jesus three times. There was nothing wrong with a hungry Man fixing himself something to eat, or with God demonstrating His power, or the goal that every knee should bow before Jesus. But the methods that the devil offered would have placed Jesus under Satan's power, and the same is true of our conflict with evil.

The clearer we become about the fact of our struggle, the more certain we must be of our weapons. The way of love is all that Jesus has given us. We are to overcome evil with good.

But, some may ask, what relationship does this have to contemporary Christian communities? Certainly none are in danger of following the Munsterites, that Sixteenth-Century community that actually chose to create an army to protect itself from persecution. No, I'm not aware of any community where that's likely at this time. But then things are still pretty stable. There are places where things are difficult, but the Lord provides. For instance, the People of God community in Beirut, Lebanon, faced a difficult situation as fighting spread through the streets of their city, confining them to their buildings and cutting off most municipal services. For a while they evacuated several of their people, but after several months they felt the Lord wanted them to return to the center of the struggle as a testimony and an arm of service for the Lord. So far the Lord has seen fit to protect them from injury and death, but the time may come when He may ask them to die. The temptation to look for some source of physical protection could increase for them—or for us. Most of us know so little of what it means to suffer and have such confused ideas about our "rights" that we could panic if we were faced with a truly tough situation.

There are also many more subtle ways in which we benefit by force and power even now. We needn't become dropouts or immobilized by guilt, but we should be open to hearing the Lord about how we rely on or relate to civic force, national and international economic force, political and military force.

In the last few years Reba Place Fellowship has been challenged to hear the Lord about its political influence in the neighborhood. In most of the recent local elections the candidates have had to have the support of the Fellowship in order to win. Occasionally this has been true for even larger contests. For instance, had the Fellowship voted for his opponent, Abner Mikva would not have gone to the U.S. Congress this term. Of course any other group our size could have had the same effect because the race was so close. But in this day of disintegration there aren't many groups with such a self-conscious unity. And that has caused us to reflect on the implications of the force we hold.

We've realized that our economic influence also has an impact. When the Fellowship food budget is about $10,000 per month and most of the household managers shop at the same places, it has an impact even on a large chain market. So what do we do with that power? Do we diversify and shop at different places so we don't have it? Do we stay at the same store and demand that the market deliver reasonable prices and good quality? Should we use the power for the benefit of the United Farm Workers and demand that the store carry Union produce only? Do we say nothing, but change if service gets bad? So far we've hesitated to use that power in any intentional way, but it is there and sometimes has its effect on local businessmen.

All of these questions about how we participate in and relate to this world's system require a prayerful search of what it means to be the Peaceful Army of our Lord's love. It is not enough to inherit the ethics of an individualistic Christianity which was unconscious of God's desire for His body. To do so without testing Scripture is to put new wine in old wine skins. As we allow the Spirit to renew and reform us into a lively body, as coordinated as a disciplined army, we must become equally responsible. What will be our "Code of Conduct"? I would like to offer five principles from the Scriptures.

1. *Love your enemies.* "Do not resist the one who is evil. But if any one strikes you on the right cheek, turn to him the other also; and if anyone would sue you and take your coat, let him have your cloak as well; and if anyone forces you to go one mile, go with him two miles. Give to him who begs from you, and do not refuse him who would borrow from you. . . . I say to you, Love your enemies and pray for those who persecute you, so that you may be sons of your Father who is in heaven" (Matt. 5:39-44).

2. *Expect to suffer as a Christian and on behalf of others.* "If when you do right and suffer for it you take it patiently, you have God's approval. For to this you have been called, because Christ also suffered for you, leaving you an example, that you should follow in his steps. He committed no sin; no guile was found on his lips. When he was reviled, he did not revile in return; when he suffered, he did not threaten" (1 Pet. 2:20-23). "Beloved, do not be surprised at the fiery ordeal which comes upon you to prove you, as though something strange were happening to you. But rejoice insofar as you share Christ's sufferings, that you may also rejoice and be glad when His glory is revealed" (1 Pet. 4:12, 13). "By this we know love, that he laid down his life for us; and we ought to lay down our lives for the brethren" (1 John 3:16).

3. *We are foreigners, living in this world's system, and we should avoid its ways.* "What causes wars, and what causes fighting among you? Is it not your passions

that are at war in your members? You desire and
do not have; so you kill. And you covet and cannot
obtain; so you fight and wage war. ... Unfaithful creatures! Do you not know that friendship with the world
is enmity with God? Therefore whoever wishes to be
a friend of the world makes himself an enemy of God"
(James 4:1-4). "You are a chosen race, a royal priesthood, a holy nation, God's own people. ... Once you
were no people, but now you are God's people. ... I
beseech you as aliens and exiles to abstain from the
passions of the flesh that wage war against your soul.
Maintain good conduct among the Gentiles" (1 Pet.
2:9-12).

4. *Obey all authorities unless they are requiring you
to disobey God. Then suffer the consequences of obedience to God because "we must obey God rather
than man."* "Be subject for the Lord's sake to every
human institution, whether it be to the emperor as su-
preme, or to governors as sent by Him to punish those
who do wrong and to praise those who do right. For
it is God's will that by doing right you should put to
silence the ignorance of foolish men. Live as free men,
yet without using your freedom as a pretext for evil;
but live as servants of God. Honor all men. Love the
brotherhood. Fear God. Honor the emperor" (1 Pet.
2:12-17).

5. *Avoid this world's weapons of violence and force.
They are not powerful enough, and to stoop to using
them is to betray our Lord's way of love.* "Though
we live in the world we are not carrying on a worldly
war, for the weapons of our warfare are not worldly
but have divine power to destroy strongholds" (2 Cor.
10:4). "For we are not contending against flesh and
blood, but against the principalities, against the powers,
against the world rulers of this present darkness,
against the spiritual hosts of wickedness in the heavenly places" (Eph. 6:12). "If my kingship were of this
world, my servants would fight ... but my kingship
is not from the world" (John 18:36).

Rejection of these principles among Christians sometimes comes as the result of an imagined duty to

defend freedom and wipe out tyranny. If we are not
to fight for ourselves, aren't we at least justified in
fighting for innocent others, democracy, or some other
noble goal? But such high ideals are always the excuses
for war. No one ever admits that the true causes of
conflict are just what James said they were in 4:2:
greed, envy and ambition. However, the ideals of defending freedom constitute a powerful point because
they appeal to the virtue of compassion. There is oppression and injustice in this world, but the question is—
what is the Kingdom way to confront or alleviate it?

Jesus certainly faced the same question. His people
suffered under a government so cruel that the slaughter
of innocent babies after His birth was such a trifling
episode in comparison to the many other bloody deeds
of the Romans that it was not mentioned in the gory
records of the historian Josephus. The Roman oppression had already inspired many to join the Zealot resistance. They could have been the core of an army if
Jesus would have chosen to lead them. His triumphant
entry proved His popular support for that cause. Why
didn't He strike? Didn't He care? Would it have
been futile? Or maybe, maybe He did strike with other
weapons and methods. I think that's what happened,
and I believe He won! Praise God, the victory has been
won, and we can afford to live accordingly.

But many of us are impatient. We do not want to
leave vengeance to the Lord and His way and timing.
And so we look for excuses for why He did not mean
what He said in His Word. The Old Testament is one
of the most frequent things that people point to to suggest that God must have accepted killing and violence.
However, the Old Testament does not offer any *ap-
plicable* ethic for war, nor for the just war theoretician
or even the crusader. God's instructions as understood
and recorded in the Old Testament range from complete
passivity to the absolute annihilation of men, women,
children, babies, animals, buildings—everything. God
was not trying to communicate an ethic on war in the
Old Testament. The New Testament, on the other hand,
does offer principles, the principles of peace and sac-

rifice. We should see the Old in light of the New.

There are other questions and other passages to consider. I had to spend a very long time in Bible study and prayer before I was clearly convicted of what the Lord wanted. Five books might be helpful in reviewing many of the Scriptures and questions. They are: *The Politics of Jesus* by John Howard Yoder, *Violence* by Jacques Ellul, *The New Testament Basis of Pacifism* by G. H. C. Macgregor, *War, Peace and Nonresistance* by Guy Franklin Hershberger, and *Victory Over Violence* by Martin Hengel.

It is easy to dismiss the issue of peace as having no immediate relevance—the United States is not currently at war and many Christians are well insulated from domestic violence. But those privileges might not always be ours, and the Lord wants to prepare us in two ways. He wants to give us practice on things that are our size, like responding peacefully to personal threats.

Summer has begun while I've been working on this book, and in our densely populated neighborhood, hot weather means a lot of street action and tension. Two doors down a gang of teenagers have commandeered the front porch of a non-Fellowship building. None of the kids live there, but often as many as 20 gather and make a terrible racket until well after midnight. The residents of the building are afraid and unable to do anything. Their yard and shrubs have been trampled, the new paint on the building is filthy and written on; personal items have been stolen or destroyed. The kids insult and intimidate passersby and have sometimes refused to move so the people who live in the building can go up the steps. The kids have threatened to shoot or "cut" anybody who messes with them. Most of it is just talk, but there is a way that they jack each other up and dare each other into behavior that's really serious. The girls can effectively taunt the guys with: "Are you going to let that man tell you what to do?" when someone tries to speak to them about their behavior.

One Saturday, after a lot of abuse to one of the

residents of the building, the police came. I thought the man had called them himself, but he disappeared into his apartment, possibly not wanting to be identified as the caller. The kids scattered the moment the police came around the corner. I finally went over to talk to the police.

When the police left, the kids quickly regrouped. They thought I'd called the police and immediately began declaring how they were going to get even by bricking our windows or something.

Later in the afternoon when a few of the folks from our household were sitting out in the backyard and my baby daughter was running around, a barrage of a half dozen stones crashed around us. Another brother and I ran down the alley to try and catch the kids. All but a couple ran off before we got there. I grabbed the biggest one and backed him up to the fence and began to give him a verbal third degree to force him to identify who threw the stones. He wouldn't tell.

Later that night I found myself really depressed. I kept being shocked by the fantasy scenarios going through my mind. My fantasies didn't involve plans to call the police or organize the neighborhood or contact the parents or some other sensible approach. I wanted to crack some heads. In my mind I distanced myself from those kids as God's children who needed some care and discipline, and they began to feel like the "enemy." My anger was so great that at every idle moment my mind drifted back to the afternoon and the rage I wanted to vent. I was hooked.

Finally, I just had to confess to the Lord how totally I was failing in an area I deeply wanted to follow Him. I felt like an utter fool, and as I opened myself to the Lord that proved to be the major source of my anger. I hadn't shown those kids a thing in their terms, and I hadn't shown them any reflection of the Kingdom, either. All I wanted was revenge for my crushed pride and the danger they had caused.

That kind of anger is a long way from what I was thinking when I was riding around in the back of the army truck on the West Side. But my family and I weren't personally threatened then. What happened Saturday is like homework. The Lord explains principles in a class where we can hear them, but then He wants us to do a little homework on our hearts where we can practice putting them into effect.

Such experiences over the years make me realize just how far from peace I am by nature, and how much healing I need. Other folks may have an easy time following Jesus down that path, but not me. I must rely again and again on the Lord's grace that accepts me just the way I am, then leads me to a desire to change.

I sometimes imagine that it might be easier to be peaceful in a war or even if I were being robbed by someone who had a definite grievance or objective. I don't know. All I know is that faithfulness in the little issues that the Lord allows us to face will strengthen us and give us experience to be faithful in the larger ones if we are ever called upon to face them.

I don't think we can be too sure that we wouldn't resort to direct violence in a big way if we have not allowed the Lord to convict us of it or if we have no qualms about using it in little ways of personal confrontation, or through indirect violence such as intimidating politics, support of the military, benefiting from long-distance oppression, etc. Now is the time to establish the foundation. "He who is faithful in a very little is faithful also in much; and he who is dishonest in a very little is dishonest in much" (Luke 16:10).

6

Before Governors and Councils

The People of Praise community in South Bend, Indiana, owns a nine-story hotel. On the ninth floor there is a large household. On the first floor there is a Christian bookstore and a small restaurant serviced by community members and open to the public. The other floors house many ministry projects, meeting rooms, offices and guest space for frequent conferences.

I was having lunch in the restaurant with Paul DeCelles, one of the head coordinators of the community, when he leaned over to me and said, "See those two men who came through the door? The one on the right is the mayor; the other man is the city attorney."

"Do they eat here often?" I asked.

"I've never seen them in here before," Paul said. "In fact, I don't know them personally."

After we finished eating, we went over to their table. Paul introduced himself and welcomed them. I excused myself after a few minutes, and Paul had the opportunity to show the men through the hotel and give a clear witness about what they were doing and why they were doing it.

It was no major event in itself, just a wise mayor wanting to know what was going on with this group of people which kept growing and growing, and could import 150 people into the city in a few weeks' time. But it was an example of one of the kinds of ways that a very radical Christian life-style can be a testimony for the Gospel. Total dedication to anything other than a person's self-interest is peculiar, and when it takes place among a group of people, there is cause for others to want to know what is happening.

Jesus instructed us about this: "Take heed to yourselves; for they will deliver you up to councils; ... and you will stand before governors and kings for my sake, to bear testimony before them.... And when they bring you to trial and deliver you up, do not be anxious beforehand what you are to say; but say whatever is given you in that hour, for it is not you who speak, but the Holy Spirit" (Mark 13:9-13).

At Reba Place Fellowship we have had a good deal of interaction with the city government over zoning for our extended-family households. Evanston's zoning laws, like those of most cities, did not make provision for extended-family living arrangements. Usually there can be no more than two or three unrelated adults living in the same dwelling. That has changed now. After three years of work with the City Council and its various sub-committees, the City now recognizes a new type of family, a type (C) family. It gives a legal classification for extended family households such as those in our Christian community. But the story of the many times we have been able to stand humbly before the City Council and give testimony to the ministry the Lord has given us and the basis in Him for our life is truly worth telling.

The whole process started in the summer of 1973 when we got a notice on a couple of our households informing us that we were out of compliance with the City ordinance. At that time we didn't quite know what to do, and so we contacted an attorney with the ACLU. He advised us that we should go into Federal Court and stop the whole thing. The ACLU expressed interest in handling the case. However, their lawyer suggested that first we'd better do a little more research.

Timothy Jost, one of our members, was in law school at the time, so he inquired among his professors as to who would be a good zoning lawyer in Chicago. They recommended Ross, Hardies, O'Keefe, Babcock and Parsons—one of the best zoning law firms in the country. When Timothy called, he was referred to one of their lawyers who was an Evanston resident and already knew about the Fellowship. After the first consultation the firm agreed to take on our case— not for their usual $100 per hour, but for free.

Instead of going right to court, it seemed best to explore all the possible ways of working things out within the City Council. So we went to the first hearings, not knowing what would happen. As it turned out, one of the reasons that the City had sent us notice on our houses was that the City had another case before it involving a group of young people trying to live communally elsewhere in the city. Their situation had created complaints among their neighbors, and when the City followed up on those complaints, the young people pointed out that the City had been permitting Reba Place Fellowship to live together in households for years. That was actually true. The City had been ignoring our violations because our neighbors appreciated our presence. However, when the young people pointed out that inconsistency, the City had to respond with equal application of their rules.

The hearing started out with the young people presenting their case, but there was a great deal of hostility. Several of their neighbors were present and angry and the arguing went on for a couple of hours. The Zoning Amendments Committee members were getting fed up with the whole thing. Finally, that ended and Reba Place Fellowship was called upon to testify. Virgil Vogt, one of our elders, just shared for a while what our life was like and how we felt that the Lord had called us to use extended family households as effective tools for ministry and fellowship. He didn't hesitate at all to declare that our motivation was out of love and obedience to Jesus Christ.

The attorney that the Lord had given us from such a well-known firm also spoke in our behalf as did the pastor from the local First Baptist Church; Russ Barta, a sociologist who lives right in our neighborhood; Don Borah, the president of the local neighborhood association; and a local realtor. A peace settled into the room, and there was a dramatic change of attitude on the part of the committee members. From that time on they were willing to work with us in an attempt to see if there were some way they could accommodate our needs.

Not all of them thought it was a good idea for the City to allow us to continue living as we were, but they were willing to consider it with an open mind. Of course there were hundreds of things to be researched and nearly three years of meetings with various committees and finally the whole City Council before an amendment was approved as law. Both of our aldermen supported us throughout the entire process as we tried again and again to come up with wordings that would allow us to do what the Lord had called us to do while protecting the City from irresponsible living arrangements.

As far as we knew this was the only ordinance of its kind in the country explicitly permitting households. We felt that there was value in taking advantage of this time when our neighbors and City government supported us to establish not only permission but protection under the law that might be used as a precedent by other communities in their relations with the cities in which they live.

If you can get through the "legalese," the amendments read as follows: Under the section defining "family" there is now a new subsection.

(C) A group of two (2) or more persons containing within it one (1) or more families, as defined above, including a husband and wife married to one another and their children, as well as adults, living together in a dwelling unit as a single housekeeping unit and management, in premises in which the adult occupants are affiliated with a bona-fide not-for-profit corporation organized for religious purposes chartered by the State of Illinois which owns or rents the property and has been in existence for at least five (5) years prior to seeking certification by the Director of Inspections and Permits as hereinafter provided, provided that in no case shall the total occupancy of the dwelling unit exceed two (2) persons per bedroom, nor shall the premises be utilized for religious

services open to the public or otherwise used as places of public assembly.

In order to qualify for certification we must now go through the following application procedure:

Upon written application to the Director of Inspections and Permits, certification of approval shall be issued for occupancy of a dwelling unit by a type (C) family in all districts where dwelling units are allowed, except R-1 and R-2, provided that the applicant establishes that the occupancy conforms with the definition of a type (C) family. The members of a type (C) family household shall not keep or store more than one (1) motor vehicle for each such dwelling unit or for each off-street parking space lawfully existing in connection with such dwelling unit, whichever is greater. Certification will be revoked at any time the occupancy or off-street parking no longer conforms to the definition of a type (C) family, or if, upon reasonable review, a request for current records is not answered so as to establish that the type of ownership complies with the definition of a type (C) family.

To those of us who are not familiar with how laws are drafted and worded these rulings may seem very complex and ominous. It may sound like there are so many clauses that we have very little freedom or could lose our permits at any time because of some technicality. But that's not really the case. We came to see that there is good reason for each restriction.

For instance, Evanston is a university town and it is also an active center for various sects—Hare Krishna, Scientology, The Way, etc.—so the ruling was worded so that a household would need to be built around a natural family as the core and would not be operated as a dorm or rooming house. The household is to be sponsored by a religious group (not a fraternity) that has been in existence long enough to be stable and responsible. Of course, a sect might be able to meet those requirements, in which case the City could not object. But at least the City would be protected from the more irresponsible ventures.

The restriction on the number of people according to the size of the house was very reasonable. There are health and safety factors that we all support. And no neighborhood would appreciate a household that was an excuse for parking a lot of cars on the street.

The restriction on holding religious services open to the public seemed strange at first until we realized that you can't turn a private home into a public meeting place anyway. That doesn't mean that you can't have a Bible study or prayer meeting in your living room to which you invite friends. And it doesn't restrict our basic freedom of assembly. The issue is that *public meeting* halls must meet some code requirements that are related to basic safety; adequate restrooms must be provided, exit signs, panic bars on the doors, parking spaces, etc.

We were not any more interested in fostering irresponsible living situations than the City was, so we were glad to work with them in carefully wording the law. And now we even have the protection of the law. Whereas in the past sympathetic officials were overlooking ways that we didn't comply with the code thereby allowing us to exist, we are now entitled to exist and receive a permit, provided we meet the requirements. And should the climate of sympathy cool among the officials, they cannot arbitrarily close our households.

We have been very grateful for being in the same situation with our neighbors that the first church faced, "having favor with all the people" (Acts 2:47). And yet that did not last indefinitely with them and may not be ours forever either. The day may come when we face opposition and hostility. The clearer our light shines, the more contrast there will be with the worldly culture. And at some point that contrast may become a conflict with legal implications. We never want to invite that kind of tension and want to take great pains to work things out as we did over the zoning issue. Living in a household is not a central part of our faith or doctrine. But it is a central tool in the ministry of about half our people. It seemed to be a tool that the Lord had given us, and we were not ready to abandon it easily.

In the future more Christian communities may face disputes over zoning, education, participation in war or other issues just as early Christians were called before the councils over elements of their lives and ministry. But we should not shy away from that. It can be a great opportunity to speak the Gospel before those who would have no other occasion to hear us out. Whether the Lord uses that testimony to broaden our freedom and protection or not is His business. We are called to be faithful and "serve God rather than man." In the process we can witness for our Lord.

Part Two

Internal Organization

7

Is There Anarchy in Narnia?

In his enchanting series, *The Chronicles of Narnia*, C. S. Lewis creates a detailed world of beauty, archetypal conflicts and Christian analogies that captivate the imagination. *Something* in the Land of Narnia resonates with the human spirit and becomes a fetching fantasy, a dream of the way things ought to be.

This popularity is somewhat paradoxical because many people fail to notice that this fantasy world is based on a kind of order that they vigorously resist in their daily lives. You would think that a person would consciously attempt to move his life toward the ideals he values in his dreams, but many of us live by and publicly advocate an independence that would be anarchy in Narnia. In Narnia the people (such as the Dwarfs) who do their own thing apart from the authority and order of Peter, High King of Narnia, and his helpers are not models of benign individualism; they are the rebels. Knowingly or unknowingly, demon or dupe, they fight against the Christ figure Aslan, and even Aslan's great Father, Emperor-beyond-the-sea.

The parallel to the Kingdom of God is clear. The Lord did not ascend to heaven without establishing a regent, and it was His church, filled with the power of His Spirit. Yet the worldly spirit of individualism has so influenced many Christians that they seldom imagine that they might be living in spiritual anarchy.

Our redemption is to free us from slavery to sin and selfishness and to enable us to re-enter the Kingdom of God, ready and able to do His will. But we often envision the "Lord's will" as the path of greatest success. We like to think that the "wonderful plan for our life" is the one that will bring us the most rewards. Sometimes evangelism is based on this by holding up the testimonies of successful businessmen, athletes or entertainment stars in a way that makes it appear that worldly success is the reward for faith. That approach encourages a very self-centered religion, similar to the basis of this world's system. The Apostle James said, "You ask and do not receive, because you ask wrongly, to spend it on your passions. Unfaithful creatures! Do you not know that friendship with the world is enmity with God?" (James 4:3, 4). The "world" here is the world's system of self-serving. James is not making a distinction between being an ethical self-server and an unethical one. The world's system is that which began with Adam when he chose to make his own decisions about what was best for him apart from God's counsel. Wherever that is being duplicated, it is a function of this world's system, whether it is a child, a criminal, or a very principled businessman. That is why Paul could write: "All have sinned." Certainly this world's system functions more smoothly when it is based on ethics which are reflections of God's character such as honesty, compassion and justice. But it is still the world's system, and that is why the solution that James offers is, "Submit yourselves therefore to God" (James 4:7 ff.).

Most Christians imagine that they *would* submit to the Lord if He were to come bodily to them and give them a directive, and many of us might. But discovering the Lord's will is not so simple, and if we are honest, we usually have to admit that our attempts to hear His voice are sometimes clouded by our own ambitions, fears, and prejudices. How do we deal with that problem?

I believe that the main purpose for the existence of the church is so that Jesus can satisfy our daily need to discover and do God's will and discover and receive God's love.

However, not every church embodies this as its purpose. It is possible to be an active, evangelistic, doctrinally correct, devoted group of believers without fulfilling Christ's intention for His church. He intended His church to be an experience of "Emmanuel," God with us, so that each of us can personally encounter the authority of the Lord to discover His will in our lives. The rich meaning in the term "the body of Christ" is seen in this role of the church. In the church we face Christ's body filled by His Spirit. Until Christ's return nothing will be more tangible. The church is not just Christ's fan club for worship or His class for teaching or His representatives for action and witness or His friends for fellowship. It is Christ's contemporary presence in the world.

There is no need for spiritual anarchy to exist until Jesus returns. He is with us even now in His church. Because of the indwelling of His spirit, His church is even more than a regent. It is Emmanuel!

Christ was trying to wean the disciples off the necessity of His physical presence and onto the reality of Emmanuel as the church when He said, "Yet a little while I am with you. . . . Where I am going you cannot come. A new commandment I give to you, that you love one another" (John 13:33, 34).

When Peter heard that, he wasn't interested in being weaned off Christ's physical presence. He boasted of his love and loyalty for Jesus and said, "Lord, why cannot I follow you now? I will lay down my life for you."

But later that night Christ was arrested, and before morning Peter denied Him three times as Jesus had predicted. After His resurrection, Christ confronted Peter again on the same issue, asking three times, "Do you love me?" And three times Peter tried to answer yes, finally saying, "Lord, you know everything; you know that I love you." But Jesus said to him, "Tend to my sheep" (John 21:15-17).

Jesus was not trying to humiliate Peter for his mistake by asking three times. Peter did love Jesus, and Jesus knew it. But what Peter hadn't learned was *how* Christ wished him to express that love. Peter hadn't learned the significance of the new commandment to love one another. The moment Christ left physically, Peter went back to his private agenda of fishing—serving himself as he thought best. It was no *evil* task Peter turned to; it was just a *private* task apart from God's will. He hadn't learned that he could continue relating to Jesus by relating to His body, the church.

The time was almost past when Jesus would be with His disciples in person. But He would be there (and even more powerfully, He promised) in their midst. It is significant that later after Jesus did ascend, the apostles pointed to the obvious unity of the church as proof of the resurrection. They didn't rely on an empty tomb, but on the lively assembled body. And that was the fulfillment of Jesus' prayer: "I pray that they may all be one; even as thou, Father, art in me, and I in thee, that they also may be in us, so that the world may believe that thou hast sent me" (John 17:20, 21).

It was with this kind of a relationship in mind that the Lord delegated His authority to the church in the first place. It is almost shocking to realize the significance of the authority that Jesus passed on to the church in saying, "As the Father has sent me, even so I send you. . . . If you forgive the sins of any, they are forgiven; if you retain the sins of any, they are retained" (John 20:21, 23).

Paul was nearly overwhelmed as he considered the seriousness of this responsibility. "Who is sufficient for these things?" he asks after noting that we are the essence of Christ both to other believers and to the world. To those who are looking to God we are a sweet aroma, but those who reject God find us as distasteful as they found Jesus. (See 2 Cor. 14-17.) As the church refocuses its identity and authority, it increasingly may become an anathema within the world's system.

Who among us, even who collectively, is competent to claim to be such total agents of Christ?

Certainly none of us. Paul says, "Not that we are competent ourselves to claim anything as coming from us; our competence is from God, who has made us competent to be ministers of a new covenant. For what we preach is not ourselves, but Jesus Christ as Lord with ourselves as your servants for Jesus' sake" (2 Cor. 3:5, 6; 4:5). God has shown His wisdom in not choosing a personally competent representative or in making us perfect. "We have this treasure in earthen vessels, to show that the transcendent power belongs to God and not to us" (2 Cor. 4:7). But it is divine power nonetheless—the very authority of Christ himself.

"We are ambassadors for Christ, God making his appeal through us. . . . For we are the temple of the living God; as God said, 'I will live in them and move among them, and I will be their God, and they shall be my people' " (2 Cor. 5:20; 6:16, 17).

There is a real difference between being *a people of God* and being *persons for God.* Persons for God are free-lance Christians with the attitude of "just me and God," and that attitude reproduces the confused conditions of Israel recorded at the end of the book of Judges: "In those days there was no king in Israel; every man did what was right in his own eyes." They had the Law and actually God was their King if they would have recognized His authority in the prophets and the elders of the congregation. But they didn't, not in a unifying way, and so there was a kind of pious anarchy similar to recent conditions among many Christians.

The claim that "Jesus is Lord" must move from an individualistic idea to the practical reality of recognizing that authority as it reaches us through His channel, the church, or else we are left with every man doing what is right in his own eyes. Jesus said, "He who receives any one whom I send receives me; and he who receives me receives him who sent me" (John 13:20.

The Spirit was wise in inspiring the writers of Scripture to use the analogy of the body to describe how

the church should function. We all know when our body
is not working right. If we sleep in the wrong position,
our arm can "fall asleep" and be unresponsive when
we awake. We know that that's not the way it is supposed to work. Our arm should move out when we
tell it to so that the fingers can pick up our shoe and
put it on. The body of Christ should be just as responsive
and well coordinated. Every congregation should reflect
the unity we expect from our physical bodies. And,
likewise, the congregations should be fitted together
as members of the universal body of Christ.

The body of Christ, the church, is supposed to perform tasks that many people envision in individualistic
terms. For instance, it is in the context of the body
that we are primarily built up for ministry, attain unity,
attain the knowledge of the Son of God, develop maturity, and are protected from confusion about what to
believe (Eph. 4:12-14). So often those are functions that
people attempt to do pretty much on their own. They
go off to school by themselves because they think that
they would like to enter some ministry. They decide
on their own what to believe according to what is most
persuasive to their mind. This individualistic influence
on the church has fragmented it far beyond the area
of fundamental difference in faith. And it has fragmented the individual, broken relationships, alienated
people from a sense of belonging, and been the source
of many emotional problems among believers.

A people of God who are functioning as a coordinated
body of Christ can be helping people discover God's
will for their jobs, where they should live, which ministry tasks to perform, where the money goes, whom
to marry and how to spend their time. Does that mean
that no one makes any personal decisions? No, not
necessarily. The body may delegate responsibilities as
Christ sees fit. Certainly the nerves in a hand provide
a lot of information to the brain about how the hand
picks up a cup, but the hand doesn't act alone. And
likewise a person may be given the responsibility of
determining how most of the money is spent that comes
to him, not because it is his, which is our natural at-

titude, but because it has been decided that he should be steward over it.

We've all read spy stories of a team of undercover agents that are organized in an area to fulfill a particular task. Each detail in the lives of the team's members is important if it affects the objectives of the team: where they each live and work, whether one falls in love and wants to get married, whether another one drinks too much or talks too much. If they are ultimately committed to the cause, there is no "private" business among them.

The body of Christ is similarly organized into teams. We are not undercover agents, but uncovered agents. Our ranks are organized into local church groups, and within each group there are leaders gifted to govern and guide that team in the fulfillment of God's plan. Ephesians 4:11 identifies the roles of some of those leaders as apostles, prophets, evangelists, pastors, and teachers. Where such clear coordination and commitment operate, the church can be very effective.

The impact of what it is like to be this personally submitted hit me one day as I considered something that happened to the Apostle Paul during his ministry. The story is recorded in two places, Acts 15:1-35 and Galatians 1:11—2:10. In Galatians Paul speaks more personally of how the situation affected him. In chapter one he reviews how he was trained by Christ himself in some supernatural way over a three-year period. One aspect of the gospel that Christ revealed to him was that the Gentile converts did not have to adhere to all the requirements of the law—circumcision in particular. This message, Paul claimed, came from Jesus alone and was not influenced by any man. He taught this for 14 years, but there developed such a controversy with the Judaizers, who felt every detail of the law should be enforced, that Paul took Titus and went to Jerusalem to settle the issue.

The instruction in submission comes from the way Paul acted. Jerusalem was the mother church to which he felt accountable. And he reported, "I laid before them the gospel which I preached among the Gentiles,

lest somehow I should be running or had run in vain."
Paul's integrity insists that if they had not been able
to affirm his message, he would have changed it.

Now that's dramatic submission. There was a man
with 14 years of very successful ministry behind him.
He was highly respected, and he was absolutely convinced that Jesus himself gave him a message of freedom to preach. But he was willing to have it tested
by the other Apostles. As it turned out, the leaders
in Jerusalem were able to confirm Paul's understanding, give him their blessing, and send him and Titus
on their way.

We can also trust our lives to the body in the same
way. The Lord will not fail us. If He has indeed directed
us, it will be confirmed. If the Apostle Paul felt the
need to do that over an issue he felt so certain about,
aren't we compelled by his example to lay our lives
before the church?

What About Mistakes?

Following God's pattern for church order does not
insulate us from making our own mistakes or even
from experiencing the effects of the mistakes of others.
It is not a key to escaping problems and pain. However,
it does place us in the most favorable environment
to experience God's promise that "in everything God
works for good with those who love him, who are called
according to his purpose" (Rom. 8:28).

In the pain of the moment and especially in the
pain of experiencing someone else's mistake with us,
it requires much faith to believe that God will work
it out for good; it is hard to believe that for us, it
was not an accident. This is especially true if we think
we could have avoided the mistake if we had been
in charge. Our faith can be enhanced if we remember
that God's timetable may extend over a period much
longer than we envision. We want to see the returns
of good within a few days or weeks, at the most. And
we often want the good to be counted in terms of our
own comfort or benefit, whereas the higher good may

be in terms of the advancement of the Kingdom or
of our character toughening (which may not *feel* good).

The story of Joseph's life shows three elements of
how we can deal with the mistakes others inflict upon
us. After the whole family had been united and saved
from famine, Joseph's brothers were fearful that since
their father Jacob had died, Joseph might seek revenge
for the terrible sin they committed against him by selling him into slavery. "But Joseph said to them, 'Fear
not, for am I in the place of God? As for you, you
meant evil against me; but God meant it for good,
to bring it about that many people should be kept alive,
as they are today. So do not fear; I will provide for
you and your little ones.' Thus he reassured them and
comforted them" (Gen. 50:20, 21).

This was more than a "mistake" by some well-
meaning leaders. Joseph's brothers had *intended* evil.
Yet he had processed the event so thoroughly that he
no longer had any resentment toward them. How did
he do it? Joseph's process had included the understanding that the good that God had intended was a
broader good than his personal comfort. It was true
that at that moment he was enjoying the benefits of
Egypt's wealth, but until the famine, life with the family
would have been much better than the servitude, prison
and loneliness of Egypt. God's good plan called for
sacrifice on the part of Joseph. It was a sacrifice that
in certain terms could never be restituted—those years
were gone. Joseph accepted the fact that part of his
call was to make himself expendable. This is what Jesus
did, and Peter said, "Rejoice in so far as you share
Christ's sufferings, that you may also rejoice and be
glad when his glory is revealed" (1 Pet. 4:13).

None of us are innocent like Jesus, so along with
counting ourselves expendable we can look for our lesson in each situation. For Joseph, his lesson is not
spelled out; maybe he learned how to share God's truth
in a more humble way. When he was young, he was
a pretty cocky fellow with all his dreams. It seems
as though he might have learned something from his
experiences; at least he didn't offend Pharaoh as he

had his brothers. As a 17-year-old, Joseph started off by boasting, "Hear this dream that I have dreamed. . . ." But years later when Pharaoh asked for an interpretation, Joseph humbly answered, "It is not in me; God will give Pharaoh a favorable answer."

Also obvious in the story of Joseph was his willingness to wait for God's timing before he could even see the broader good. He waited 23 years after being sold into slavery before he realized the fact of God's purpose. And if that's not enough of a challenge to our patience and faith, Hebrews 11 lauds some other old saints who never experienced the fulfillment of God's good plan. Verse 13 says, "These all died in faith, not having received what was promised, but having seen it and greeted it from afar. . . ."

We too can keep the faith, survive mistakes, and live in trusting submission only if we will count ourselves expendable, look for our lesson, and trust God's timing and control of the matter. Without these three commitments we are bound for confusion.

8

Free Will Among a Submitted People

Our submission to the authority of Jesus as it is expressed through His church is essential if we are to say, "Jesus is Lord." However, order is not its own justification; we must seek a godly order. And a godly order is one in which our submission is voluntary and uncoerced.

Francis Schaeffer believes that much of society is past the place of merely wanting to fantasize about order. He fears that people are so frightened by the potential chaos of a modern society without ethical moorings that many people are ready to accept authoritarian governments and oppressive measures and give up freedom in order to satisfy their desire for security and prosperity. Panic cannot be the motivation for the renewal of the church as God's Kingdom under His government. God has asked us to give up our independence in order to be molded into the image of His Son and be coordinated as His functioning body, but He wants us to retain our freedom.

That may sound impossible to the person who has never willingly submitted. He may think that to surrender his independence is to lose his freedom. But the Lord is gathering a people who are freely willing to serve Him. That is the way we begin our walk with the Lord, and care must be taken to be sure each believer continues in that spirit. If we want to walk with Jesus, we must walk where He leads, but we are never *forced* to walk with Him.

The Bible promises that a time will come when "at

82

the name of Jesus every knee should bow, in heaven
and on earth and under the earth, and every tongue
confess that Jesus Christ is Lord, to the glory of God
the Father" (Phil. 2:10, 11). How that is finally to be
brought about and what it will mean is a mystery in
the mind of God, but we have not been called to revoke
the free choice that God has granted man.

However, within the context of the church the balance between submission and free will has not been
automatically preserved. When some people think about
giving themselves to a more total church life, they
become worried that some of the tragic mistakes of
church history will be repeated and they will be the
recipients of abusive authority. This is a very understandable fear; there is a risk in the exercise of authority. Where there is little power, there is little potential
for good or evil, but where there is great power, there
is both a greater opportunity for good and an accompanying possibility that mistakes may have serious consequences. Some people have preferred to keep the
church weak and hopefully innocent. We are hearing
the Lord call us to take a more courageous approach
and to let His Spirit move in power in our midst. But
we want to acknowledge the risks and search for the
Lord's way through them.

In many communities members make promises to
the Lord and to each other in the form of a covenant
which helps them get through temporary moments of
doubt and confusion. Those covenants are very useful.
But if the person's *heart* does not soon return to affirm
the commitment of his past, resentments can build.
Even when no pressure is intended, a person may comply with a community decision which may be against
his will simply because he has invested so much of
himself in the life of the community that he won't risk
a confrontation that may lead to a deadlock or separation. So he swallows his disagreement, adds one more
incident to his list of resentments and tries to go on.
Unfortunately, such a break in communication and trust
plays a part in the story of most people who leave
community. When that happens, it doesn't necessarily

mean that the community was at fault or had the habit of bringing coercive pressure to bear on its members, but somehow the person's free will was not operating in a healthy way in the context of his own submission.

Before we try to discuss some ways in which we can live in a healthy balance, it might be good to review a few items from the experience of church history, even though they seem far removed, to get a perspective on the problem. The early Anabaptists had a unique stake in pursuing the search for balance. They were the frequent targets of coercion by other church groups intent on changing them against their will. In thousands of instances this meant torture and death. Still, they never lost sight of the necessity of discipline in the body of Christ. One of their prime motivations for wanting to have a believers' church was so that they could maintain discipline without the need for force— people participated because they wanted to do so. For them that meant that they never wanted to force the determined rebel to conform but wanted to help the willing person live righteously. They tried to follow Paul's advice to "be at peace among yourselves ... admonish the idlers, encourage the fainthearted, help the weak, be patient with them all. See that none of you repays evil for evil, but always seek to do good to one another and to all" (1 Thess. 5:13-15). They knew the Lord wanted His people to be a holy people, so they searched for the scriptural means of giving and receiving correction without employing worldly force.

The conclusion of the Anabaptists was that spiritual authority was all that the church should use, and that, in fact, spiritual weapons were ultimately the most powerful means for redemption. Matthew 18:15-17 and 1 Corinthians 5:1-5 became their examples for church discipline. Correction should be attempted privately to spare the individual any embarrassment. This would take place at least three times within ever larger circles of people until the whole church besought the person to repent. If by loving appeal they could not win their brother's free change of heart, and if his sin had been of a gross or serious sort, they would be obliged to count him as no longer a part of the fellowship. They called it the "ban." The weight of the ban was spiritual, though if the person was in a severe rebellion, he would likely disregard the spiritual consequences and only feel the social impact of the ban. There certainly was a social impact, and the force of that may have coerced some people. But it was far, far removed from the confinement, torture and executions that were otherwise common at that time.

Menno Simons, one of the early Anabaptists, did not believe that even the ban should be used to force or pressure a person. He said, "Understand correctly, no one is excommunicated or expelled by us from the communion of the brethren but those who have already separated and expelled themselves from Christ's communion." His view was that the ban should be only a very sad recognition of what already was.

Simons also took pains to teach that the ban was not to have any physical consequences. It was not to restrict the flow of necessary business, loving attention to physical needs, or even politeness. "Good manners, politeness, respectfulness, and friendliness to all people becomes all Christians.... For how can such a one be convicted, led to repentance and moved to do better by such austerity? The ban is not given to destroy but to build up."

Jesus dealt with the question of coercion and violence in Matthew 11:12. He said, "From the days of John the Baptist until now the kingdom of heaven has suffered violence, and men of violence take it by force." He was referring to the fact that the momentum of John's preaching had inspired the Zealots to step up their efforts to bring the Kingdom in by force. Jesus said that was not His way. Not only is it futile but counter-productive. It hurts the Kingdom.

Paul demonstrated the limits God placed on the church's authority in 2 Corinthians 10. There had been some nasty problems in the church that Paul had spoken to very strongly by letter. Some people in the church, familiar only with worldly responses to disobedience, apparently expected Paul to have the sinners

punished. When he hadn't done that, they thought Paul
was weak. Paul quickly pointed out that they didn't
know what they were talking about if they expected
him to act in a worldly fashion. "For though we live
in the world, we are not carrying on a worldly war,
for the weapons of our warfare are not worldly but
have divine power to destroy strongholds" (2 Cor.
10:3, 4). Earlier Paul had urged excommunication
(much in the manner of Matthew 18) for a man who
was refusing to terminate an incestual relationship.
But Paul's detractors had apparently not viewed that as
very powerful. Paul believed that it was powerful.
He also believed that the real battles took place in
wrestling with the principalities, powers, and rulers
of darkness, through prayer, fasting, preaching, teaching and righteous living. Doing what his detractors
might have counted impressive would have been entirely off the point.

Paul also says, "We are prepared to punish all
rebellion when once you have put yourselves in our
hands. . . . Our hope is rather that, as your faith
grows, we may attain a position among you greater
than ever before, but still within the limits of our
sphere" (2 Cor. 10:6, 15, NEB). The point is that we
can require nothing of a person except that to which
he willingly submits.

Laws now protect the civil rights of the individual
so that there is little risk that a problem would ever
become as serious as the mistaken applications of
church authority in history. But people can still feel
that they've been pressured into acquiescence, or
they can become afraid to speak out what they heard
the Lord telling them. How can we keep true to the
Gospel and avoid the subtle misuse of power that Satan
would draw us into? Our recognition of the danger
and commitment to honor the free will of adults is
the beginning. But there are also several aspects of
church structure and practice that aid in helping our
churches to be trustworthy. Here are a few areas for
attention.

1. All Godly Authority Proceeds from Submission

In the Gospel of John there are dozens of statements of Jesus in which He continually disavows having any authority of His own. All of His authority, everything He says and does, comes only from the Father. Repeatedly He makes the same point: "The Son can do nothing of his own accord," "I can do nothing on my own authority," "My teaching is not mine but his who sent me," "I have not come of my own accord," "I declare what I have heard," "I speak what I have seen from my Father." There seems to be no end to Jesus' effort to make that point. And it is one we should heed. If Jesus, the Holy Son of God, without sin, considered that He had no right to act except under submission to the Father, we certainly must be submitted before we dare to exercise any authority.

This principle is an important protection for the church. Much of the resistance people have to church authority stems from personal experience or reports of authority that has been abused. But authority need not be shelved just because it has been abused; the corrective is *proper* use. Each person in authority must be in submission, and that must be as active a submission as anyone else in the church experiences.

Multiple leadership is one of the ways in which church leaders can experience submission. For this to be real a leader must seek out team members who are mature and strong enough to be able to genuinely challenge him. If he pads his team with good but junior men who can't really stand up to him, he's making a joke of submission. One good test of this is to ask if challenges do happen regularly. There need not be a spirit of rebellion or controversy in the air. In fact, if there is, the whole process is not working right. But if the team members are "yes-men," they are seeking human approval of their leader, not listening to the Lord.

Another way in which leaders experience submission is by submitting to the local body. If the leaders are truly leading and hearing the Lord, there will not be very many times when they need to be corrected by the body as a whole, but it should be an option.

Recently at Reba Place the elders had scheduled a series of meetings for a visiting teacher. He was not well known, but the subject on which he was going to speak, his perspective, and his relationship with the Lord seemed to commend our investment of time. After the first session of the seminar several members of the congregation wondered what was the matter. They were getting very little out of it. At first they thought that the problem was within themselves. Hadn't the *elders* booked this teacher? However, after the second session when the teaching still fell flat, these people had a chance to test their own thoughts and responses. There was little hesitation in coming to the elders and questioning their decision. By that time the elders were also seeing the problem and were ready to terminate the series in as graceful and loving a manner as possible.

The health in that situation was that all the people in the body felt free to share their misgivings and that the elders were willing to listen and correct the situation.

In Matthew 18 Jesus reveals a foundational principle about the authority of the body. In verses 15 through 17 Jesus describes how we are to work out conflicts within the church by including increasingly larger circles of people. The point of church authority in this teaching is that Jesus reserved the most grave area of responsibility, the breaking of fellowship, for the assembled body of believers only. It is there that the responsibility finally rests. In our churches, the authority of the leadership should also be tucked back under, in submission to the body as a whole. That doesn't mean that real leadership is hobbled and unable to move out beyond the members, it doesn't infer a democracy, and it doesn't relieve the leaders of the responsibility for the flock in their care, as is mentioned in Hebrews 13:17. It does, however, fold the peak of the pyramid of authority back to a point of submission.

A third arena of submission for church leadership should be submission to some arm of the church outside the local body. This could be within a denomination to a bishop or presbytery, or it could be within a network of communities which are willing to take real responsibility for each other, or it could even be to an apostolic team overseeing the ministry in several churches. But again it needs to be real and responsible, and it should be of a quality that is recognized and respected by other branches of the church. It does no good to be in submission to some denomination which couldn't care less what one does, and it's foolish to latch onto some self-appointed apostle who is not respected or recognized by anyone else.

Submission to the church universal also should happen. One way is a willingness to receive counsel from other leaders in the church with whom there is not a formal relationship. This is mostly in terms of a teachable spirit. We must all be ready to test and learn from the wisdom and experience of others.

Jesus' example of submission to the Source of His authority is so clear and so strong that it can be said that any authority which does not come through a submitted leader is illegitimate, a thief and robber trying to climb over the wall. When Jesus said that His sheep "know his voice. A stranger they will not follow, but they will flee from him, for they do not know the voice of strangers" (John 10:4, 5), He was referring to this quality of submission so clearly evident in everything He said, in His very voice. That quality should characterize His under-shepherds.

2. Authority Must Be Fluid

A trustworthy church is one that can respond to the move of the Spirit. He is the source of effective ministry. Paul wrote to Timothy, "Don't be hasty in the laying on of hands," and he might have added, don't be afraid to lay them off either. This is another element that makes a church trustworthy. If the leadership can be removed when it is not functional, people can more freely submit themselves without the fear that they are going to be ruled by someone who is not representing the Lord.

At Reba Place persons have been called into the position of elder, served for a time, and then stepped back, half-a-dozen times over the years. There are several reasons why this has happened. We have made mistakes in confirming their leadership hastily only to discover later that the person was not properly suited for that responsibility. However, most frequently the change has come as the Lord brought the person to a new place where the role of elder was not appropriate. Sometimes the person has stepped back because it was evident that there was a need for personal growth that would be distracted by broader responsibilities.

Whatever the cause, a church has to be able to acknowledge and respond when the anointing for a task no longer applies. Some churches have traditionally dealt with that issue by having periodic elections for leaders. That method has its disadvantages. Popular vote is a poor way to "un-choose" one because it doesn't lovingly help the individual deal with the fact of the change or the reasons for change.

3. All Believers Must Know the Order of Priority for Authority

In trying to discover and follow God's will there are two extremes into which we can slip. The most natural and common is to make ourselves our own final court of appeal, listening sometimes to the advice of others but deciding for ourselves, accountable to no one. The other extreme on the spectrum is a blind obedience to everything anyone says to us with no sense of personal responsibility for discernment. But who does have the final responsibility—a member or his pastor? Is there ever a time when one shouldn't submit?

Once one has settled his own rebellion and declared his openness to receive God's direction through others, there is something more to be said. There is an order of priority in responding to authority around us. If there is ever a disagreement between the instructions of God and man, we *are* to "obey God rather than man" (Acts 5:29). That's easily said, but how is that judgment made without being tempted to claim a disagreement to justify following our own opinion?

It seems that the order of priority in testing God's will should be first Christ, then the Bible, the church, church leaders, family heads, and finally our individual discernment—from highest authority to least authority. Some Christians have tried to deal with this issue under the subject of "chain-of-command." However, the whole role of the church is often dangerously left out of those discussions. The church is supposed to play a primary part in settling disagreements about what God is saying to us. By following the process outlined in Matthew 18:15-17, which allows for a higher and higher appeal while pursuing unity rather than division, the Lord can help us settle almost any problem. This process envisions a true willingness on everyone's part to really search for what is right; it doesn't promote a blind obedience to a wooden headship.

If an individual feels the need to go against the counsel of his whole church, it should only be over something that is unequivocally clear in God's Word. That may happen, but it shouldn't happen easily. Certainly we would be obligated to disregard any instruction which would cause us to violate the historically recognized basics of the Christian faith. For instance, the Apostles' Creed collects many of the most basic components of a doctrinal or belief framework found in the Bible, and the Ten Commandments establish a skeleton for moral and ethical conduct. And there are other scriptural mandates that are clearly spelled out in the Bible. Paul expected that the Galatians were intelligent enough to figure out what the basics were when he said, "Even if we, or an angel from heaven, should preach to you a gospel contrary to that which you received, let him be accursed" (Gal. 1:8, 9). And I believe that if we are honest with ourselves, we too can decipher what are the basic truths and what are just "stupid, senseless controversies" (2 Tim. 2:23), which Paul also warned us again and again to avoid.

Peter said, "No prophecy of scripture is a matter of one's own interpretation" (2 Pet. 1:20). Therefore, where scripture is not crystal clear, where some interpretation is needed, it should not be done privately but through the church. God has given the church the binding and loosing authority to actually set the policies on the details of interpretation, and He will honor those policies in heaven and hold the members of that body accountable (Matt. 18:18). Because it happened so long ago, it is easy for us to forget that it was the church through which the Holy Spirit gave us the New Testament. The Lord honored its authority as the channel to oversee the writing, testing and selection of scriptures for the Canon we now trust as authoritative.

Though there is a divine order to authority which includes the role of the church far more actively than most modern churches recognize, the individual is endowed with a free will and does bear personal responsibility before God. The more clearly the believer understands the priority of authority, the less confusion will arise over whether he should ever not obey.

4. Individuals Must Practice Hearing the Lord

In spite of the fact that our personal impressions of the Lord's will are to be subject to the testing of the church, the church's health and ability to discern correctly will be largely determined by how well its individual members are able to hear the Lord. The preservation of the individual's free will is enhanced in a church where everyone is actively encouraged to hear the Lord for himself, not in an individualistic fashion, but as part of the process of discovering the Lord's unity for the whole body.

The most critical way in which we hear the Lord individually is through a thorough understanding of what He has said in the Bible. Expository teaching should be a steady diet so that each member of the community gains an understanding of the broad sweep of God's plan for His children throughout the ages. Also, Bible study methods should be taught so that everyone has the basic tools to conduct his personal Bible study. Then each person should be encouraged to pursue a regular pattern of Bible reading and study, expecting the Holy Spirit to teach him through the Word.

But beyond this, the Lord can speak to us directly. Jim Stringham, one of the members at Reba Place, has been very instrumental in encouraging exercises which aid us in learning to hear the Lord. Jim has suggested that each person set aside a portion of his daily devotional time to listen to the Lord—this is apart from worshiping Him, studying the Word or interceding for oneself or others. After offering a simple prayer affirming one's desire to give his whole life to the Lord, one should tell the Lord that he is listening and wants the Lord to speak to him.

Jim suggests that the Lord always has something to say to the person. Therefore, one should write down whatever comes to mind. It is important to write out those thoughts as an aid to keep the mind from wandering and as a record for testing and praise. At first one tends to think that the thoughts are insignificant or totally the product of one's own imagination, and sometimes they are. But that's the purpose of testing. In time, however, faith grows as the person experiences insights, comfort and correctives that seem beyond himself.

In my own life the Lord has used this process to teach me about himself and how we are to relate. He's drawn me closer and become much more personal. He has helped me order my day and set aside worries that were not my concern. He has guided me out of conflicts with other people and has given me direction for decisions. I think my faith that the Lord *is* able to get through to me in this method has been built most when He has challenged and corrected me in those quiet moments. It's often with a loving humor that assures me that He understands me and is on my side.

Of course, everything one hears privately from the Lord is subject to testing. The Lord never contradicts himself. What *He* says will always agree with the Bible, and it will agree with what He says to the rest of the body. If there is disunity, somebody is not hearing correctly. Maturity is becoming one with the mind of Christ not only by knowing His Word and His nature, but by letting them become a part of oneself. The new Christian is wise to share all of his journal writings with his pastor. His growth is noted as he hears more items correctly and as the content of the Lord's messages move from milk to meat. The Lord doesn't need to remind the mature Christian to get up and go to work every morning—he knows that that is the Lord's will without a discussion. As the new Christian matures, he becomes more aware of which items need testing with others and which are reasonably accurate without a formal test.

This exercise keeps our free wills healthy by helping all the believers have enough confidence in their relationship with the Lord to speak up if something does not seem right.

5. Fear Chokes Free Will

In 1 John 4:18 we read, "There is no fear in love, but perfect love casts out fear. For fear has to do with punishment, and he who fears is not perfected in love." Yet somewhere between our passion to live righteously and our frustration with not accomplishing that goal, we occasionally try shortcuts that crush the soul and leave the individual in a ceaseless anxiety about the imperfections in his behavior and spirit.

One shortcut that we can slip into is allowing competition and insecurity to develop in our midst over qualities which rate the importance or sincerity of the individual. In our churches this problem is more likely to happen in spiritual terms, but it can happen to any group. The fear that it fosters is the fear of being accused of being contrary to or inadequate for the purposes of the group. For instance, it is often rampant in extreme political movements where if one is not able to quote the latest facts and figures or use the latest jargon, he may be accused of "not caring" or even of having sympathy for the opposition. The use of one wrong word can betray one's subtle chauvinism. As a result people scramble to be more "radical" or "conservative"—adjectives which rate their security and worth in their respective groups.

Among Christians we can slip into trying to influence someone's behavior or beliefs by implying questions about his "spirituality" when he does or says something we don't like. Instead, we should speak directly to the person about his isolated behavior. We must take care that we don't allow a group dynamic of competition and insecurity to become our method of correction. Actually, striving to *be* more spiritual is like sailing into the wind; it cannot be pursued directly without being "caught in irons," the sailing term for facing directly into the wind until the ship stops, helpless. Spirituality is a quality that quietly accumulates as one tacks back and forth, following the more humble goals of *acting* in love, faith, obedience and truth.

We must reject the notion, however subtle or unspoken, that our security is tenuously dependent upon our behavior. We can be confident that we are children of God because of His gift of adopting us. When that foundation is unthreatened, the individual is free to grow, and he will actually grow faster than under the pressure of competition and insecurity.

Another fear-laden shortcut is that of using careless categories. In the course of counseling a young couple in the Fellowship, I became bewildered as to how to help them through some heavy problems in their marriage. Slowly, I began to think that the behavior of the woman corresponded to a classic psychological problem. At that time in our community several people were being diagnosed under that label. As I explored with the other elders the possibility that this woman could also have that problem, my view of the gravity of her condition deepened, and I dismissed the validity of some of her stated needs, thinking that their source was in her "problem." Before we had completed a careful diagnosis, I was treating her as though she

were in a box, and the stress of that caused her to
fulfill further symptoms of the category.

The projected therapy for that problem could have
been a long and arduous process of abreaction to "get
in touch" with the pain and primal sources for her
fear of rejection. But we never started the sessions.

By God's grace we were stopped by one of our elders
who was a woman and could understand the wife more
deeply. This elder spoke up and pointed out that the
wife's behavior was quite natural given the prejudicial
way I was treating her. And even though there was
a history to her behavior, there was a corresponding
history to the conditions that could have reasonably
produced that kind of response in anybody.

I had to repent deeply of the injustice of my careless
categorizing. Careless categories frighten people because they don't know when they are going to be put
into one or how they'd get out.

A third shortcut to growth that produces fear is the
punitive discipline. For instance, people can easily get
overextended in some areas of their lives to the neglect
of others. When that happens, balance must be restored,
and the person's pastor may have helpful suggestions
about which activities should be reduced. But the person and the rest of the community must be able to
trust or understand that there is a clear connection
between the recommended cutback and the problem,
or else it will feel punitive—a punishment rather than
a correction. There may be a logical reason why a
person is told that if he cannot care for his family
more consistently, he should consider dropping out of
the music ministry for a while. Maybe his time will
not allow both. But the specific connection between
those two functions should be made obvious. Without
adequate explanation other people may feel it was punitive and begin to fear that if they make a mistake,
they will be punished by having some unrelated, good
thing stripped away from them.

Certainly a truly punitive action should never happen in a Christian community since that is contrary to
love, but the leaders of the community are also re-

sponsible to see that there is no fear of that happening.

A seeming sincerity is generated in many people under these three and other fear-laden conditions, but it is motivated by anxious tension and insecurity. Life becomes austere and introspective (as people try to figure what's wrong with themselves) or else hectic (as they try to prove they are okay). Fear always throttles free will. The fear may be unfounded. But whether it is in the person's head or stems from problems in the community, it needs immediate attention. "Perfect love casts out fear."

6. Avoid Pastoral Grandiosity

Over the years, the occasions when we as a community have failed to adequately respect the free will of an individual have usually involved a problem of pastoral grandiosity. That may be because our main ministry is in the area of pastoral counseling—our strength becomes most vulnerable to error. By God's grace the occasions of grandiosity have not been many, and we've tried to learn all we can from our errors. We've identified at least three attitudes which sometimes arise.

The first is the fear that if we don't help the person right now, they are going to be messed up forever. That mistake forgets God's providence. The second attitude is an over-responsibility to protect an individual from the natural consequences of his errors. God can sometimes use those consequences as potent tools for correction, and the individual is often more open to change when he has no one but himself to blame. The third is a tendency to become impatient with a person's imperfections. Sometimes when a pastor slips into a fix-it mentality, he fails to see problems in their true perspective, and they may be quite minor by some standards. Impatience can also come into play over issues about which the Holy Spirit has not convicted the person. Sometimes the pastor can slip into trying to convict the person in a way that goes beyond shining the light.

These problems with grandiosity usually stem from

the commendable motives of wanting to help people follow the Lord and live joyfully, yet, at times, we fail to keep all the factors of the Christian life in balance. Should we give up and sacrifice the authority of the body of Christ because it is sometimes abused? I don't think so. We must humbly ask God to help us hold the paradox—free will among a submitted people.

9

The Character of a Leader*

It's easy to be fooled into thinking that people are mature just because they are capable. Some people are so gifted, in both a natural and a spiritual sense, that they are able to function effectively in ways that go beyond their level of maturity and personal integration. They have learned to achieve far beyond the average, but often for the wrong reasons. They may, in fact, be achieving because of immaturity. They may be performing in order to resolve a basic identity problem, or to gain a sense of acceptance or security. This is a very subtle condition, often scarcely apparent to the people themselves.

Especially for those in positions of overall leadership in the church, maturity of character is a strategic factor in the quality of leadership. On several occasions we have given leadership responsibilities in our community to people who were not able to carry through with them in a satisfactory manner. They seemed to have the necessary gifts. They were very capable. They had an authentic base of spiritual experience, having known the Lord and received much of His grace. But as they got into important pastoral responsibilities, distortions and confusion were persistently present. Prob-

*This chapter was written by Virgil Vogt, one of the elders at Reba Place Fellowship. It first appeared as an article in *Pastoral Renewal*, Aug. 1977. Copyright © *Pastoral Renewal*, 1977. P.O. Box 8617, Ann Arbor, Michigan 48107. Reprinted by permission. This monthly is available free of charge upon request. It is supported by contributions.

lems lingered or were even compounded. Deep conflicts and unresolved tensions attended their ministry.

We have learned that being able to perform certain obvious leadership activities is not enough. For pastoral leadership to be fruitful, it must come from a depth of inner security, integration, and wholeness. Leadership flows with clarity and creativity when our personal lives have been put in order before God.

It is striking that in the pastoral epistles, Paul emphasizes this point in his discussions about selecting church leaders. He seems much more concerned with qualities of personal maturity than with the ability to perform certain activities or to exercise various gifts. "For a bishop, as God's steward, must be blameless; he must not be arrogant or quick-tempered or a drunkard or violent or greedy for gain, but hospitable, a lover of goodness, master of himself, upright, holy, and self-controlled" (Titus 1:7, 8).

In considering someone for a position of pastoral leadership, we need to inquire into the depth of his Christian character. Let us try to be more specific.

A Clear Conscience

1. *A leader is one who has dealt with his own sin before the Lord.* This seems so obvious as to hardly deserve mention, but we cannot take it for granted. Paul said of himself, "I always take pains to have a clear conscience toward God and toward men" (Acts 24:16). And his requirement for other church leaders is that they "hold the mystery of the faith with a clear conscience" (1 Tim. 3:9). To readily confess our sins and receive forgiveness is a fundamental characteristic required of pastoral leaders.

This refers not only to the importance of undergoing a thorough process of forgiveness when we first come to the Lord, but includes as well the need for an ongoing process of dealing honestly with our daily failures. A leader should be one who does not cover up and make excuses for himself. If I have been dishonest in what I have said, or fudged a little in some financial transaction, it is important to confess and receive forgiveness. If I have been too rigid in holding to my view of how something should be done, or hold unresolved hostilities and resentments, it is important to confess and receive forgiveness.

Allowing the Lord to thoroughly expose and deal with sin in our own lives is a laboratory experience in which we learn how to detect and deal with sin in all its subtle and complex varieties in other people's lives.

Experiencing forgiveness for our own sin also gives us compassion for others. When we have not been honest with ourselves, we tend to respond to the sins of others with self-righteous anger. We are offended. How could anyone stoop to such a thing! But when we have come humbly before the Lord, we know that the sin of others is similar to our own. We know how easy it is to fall into sin, and how hard it is to get out of it. We know the joy of deep love and forgiveness when it comes to us in our broken condition.

Joyful and Steadfast

2. *A leader is one who has learned to deal with weakness, pain, and defeat by bringing them to the Lord.* Learning to face difficulties, without trying to deny them or run away, is an important aspect of character development. We are called in Scripture to rejoice in our sufferings (Rom. 5:3), and to be content with our weaknesses (2 Cor. 12:10). We can do this because of our relationship to the Lord. Through Him, these situations of pain and suffering are turned into moments of grace. It is through these experiences that the genuineness and beauty of His life in us are more clearly revealed.

Peter talks of this as gold being refined in the fire (1 Pet. 1:7). A leader is one who has gone through the fire and has proved genuine. This is important, because as one's leadership responsibilities grow, the heat increases! Our failures will be more far reaching, our weaknesses more obvious and distressing.

A leader should be one who has a high degree of faith and is able to accept life the way it comes, patiently bringing forth fruit. He must be able to accept other people just the way they are. As we learn to come to the Lord with our own pain, weakness, and failure, we develop a strength of character which God can use in blessing others in their moments of pain.

This strength develops into the endurance we need if we are to build anything faithfully with the Lord. It is much easier to start than to finish. This is especially true in efforts to build the Kingdom, where the resources with which we work are often of the "mustard seed" variety. No one ever tries to accomplish so much with as little as we do in the Lord's work.

"He who endures to the end will be saved" (Matt. 24:13). The term "endurance" used here could be translated more literally, "remaining under." The person who has the strength of character to "remain under" without giving up is the kind we need in positions of leadership.

A leader is one who has learned endurance in his personal life; he is able to sustain faith in Jesus through great stress, unwelcome interruptions, frequent delays, and severe setbacks.

Generous

3. *A leader is one who uses his talents and resources for others, not for his own gain.* How do we handle those spheres of life in which we are most capable and resourceful? Have we put them at the service of the Lord? Or do we eagerly use them to get as much as we can for ourselves? Have we learned to trust God for all that we need? Or is there an anxious grasping after the necessities of life?

How we approach money is a revelation regarding how we handle our talents and resources. Money is an attractive and useful thing that gives us the power for many wholesome, necessary activities. The use that a potential leader makes of money is an important clue to his character. Paul touches this point in his instruction about choosing leaders: a leader must not be "greedy for gain" or a "lover of money" (1 Tim. 3:8, 3).

Jesus encourages us to be free with our resources, to do things for others, to make friends and bless others. To have learned to do this with our money is good preparation for doing the same with spiritual resources.

A generous offering of our resources for the welfare of others springs from a confidence that our own needs will be met. Someone who is "greedy for gain" hasn't learned to trust and receive from the Lord. If we must look out for ourselves, anxious self-concern is well justified. But if the Lord provides for our every need, it is no longer necessary for us to grab at every possible benefit that becomes available in our sphere of influence. We can readily allow others to receive their share and more, confident that we will not be left empty-handed when our turn comes.

As Jeremiah so clearly addressed God's word to his helper Baruch: "And do you seek great things for yourself? Seek them not" (Jer. 45:5).

Demonstrating the Gospel

4. *A leader is one who is able to accept and affirm others warmly and affectionately.* The good news is that God loves us and gives himself for us, even while we are sinners. For people to hear this good news, it has to be demonstrated. They need to experience ready and unconditional acceptance from us. In a world starved for love and affection, we as Christian leaders must be vessels through whom the Lord's love can come to others. Encouragements, affirmation, support, affection—these make everyone thrive. Even though Christians should not depend upon the approval of others, the support and encouragement of fellow Christians can be a tremendous source of blessing and growth.

A Sense of Priorities

5. *A leader is one who knows how to manage and put in order.* This, of course, is a role that a leader

exercises within a group. But it is first of all a trait of character, something which rests on his own personal experience. A leader's ability to oversee the life and work of others is directly related to how well he has learned to manage his own life.

This requires an understanding of priorities. Jesus confronted the Pharisees because they were "straining out a gnat and swallowing a camel" (Matt. 23:24). They were unable to distinguish between weighty and lesser matters. To give each need or question its appropriate place in the total balance of life takes the wisdom of heaven. As we walk with the Lord, He teaches us, and our capacity for putting things in order grows.

Knowing how to manage also involves a sense of timing. In the plan of God, each step needs to be fulfilled at its proper moment. We have to receive God's direction so that we have a sense of His timing and know when to rest and when to work.

Forthright and Open

6. *A leader is one who has learned to be honest and straightforward.* We all know that it is a sin to deliberately say what we know to be false, and we avoid doing so most of the time. But more subtle forms of dishonesty are common.

It is easy to create an erroneous impression by what we leave unsaid. Or, as leaders, we are sometimes tempted to promise more than we can deliver. Or we may call for an unnecessary delay simply because we don't want to deal with a situation. Scripture forbids this kind of dishonesty: "Do not say to your neighbor, 'Go, and come again, tomorrow I will give it'—when you have it with you" (Prov. 3:28).

Furthermore, many of us in leadership positions are reluctant to share what is happening to us on a personal level, where our hurts, doubts, and struggles are. It is often tempting to hide our true feelings about a situation under discussion. But a person who has learned to express his thoughts and feelings honestly, even in difficult situations, has one of the essential character strengths necessary for pastoral leadership.

A Teacher at Heart

7. *A leader is one who can teach others to do things.* There are many persons who are competent at managing their own affairs, but are disinclined to ask others to do things. If put in positions of leadership, such persons tend to do too much themselves. They find it easier to overload their own schedule than to delegate work and teach others to assume a reasonable share of responsibility.

After mentioning a number of practical matters about Christian life, Paul tells Timothy to "teach and urge these duties" (1 Tim. 6:2). A leader is one who is able to instruct others in the new way of living. While this teaching is a role that leaders fulfill in the church, it is also a trait of character. Some persons are given to teaching; they find it easy; it springs naturally from their interaction with other people. You don't have to give them a classroom in order for them to teach. They teach all the time.

This aptness to teach grows, in part, out of an interest in other people and a desire to see them progressing. One who has this trait of character does not rest at ease just because he himself knows how to do something adequately. He is eager to see others learn as well.

Teaching and directing others must grow out of a mature sense of who we are. An insecure person either is afraid to assume authority over the life of another person, or tends to assume authority when it is not appropriate to do so. Being ready to teach or direct others when it is appropriate, but not hankering after it when it is inappropriate, is a valuable quality in leaders.

Obedient

8. *A good leader is one who knows how to obey.* One of the most important prerequisites for asking others to do things is a readiness to be directed ourselves.

A leader should be one to whom others find it easy to give directions.

The centurion of Capernaum gave this relationship clear expression when he said to Jesus, " 'I am a man under authority, with soldiers under me; and I say to one, "Go," and he goes, and to another, "Come," and he comes, and to my slave, "Do this," and he does it' " (Matt. 8:9). The centurion knew that his power to command and direct others grew out of the fact that he was "under authority."

To voluntarily and willingly put ourselves under authority and instruction requires a certain maturity. The immature and insecure person is afraid that his life will be destroyed or diminished by trusting others. But as we grow in our faith in God and in our assurance of His grace to us as sons, we readily submit to the proper authorities.

Able to Correct

9. *A leader is one who can correct others and resolve problems.* This is a sensitive area. Our own unresolved problems nearly always complicate situations in which we are trying to bring correction. We tend to: (1) avoid a direct approach and let the matter slide, (2) be too soft in what we require, or (3) be harsh and rigid in what we require.

All of these patterns grow out of insecurity and self-protection on our part. We can keep our distance by avoiding correction or by being harsh. Or we can come close to the other person, but avoid the pain by not requiring much change.

A good leader is one who can correct with gentleness (2 Tim. 2:25). Such correction in no way diminishes what is required or glosses over the problem. But it handles the situation with compassion for and acceptance of the person who has failed.

Servanthood

10. *A good leader must be a willing servant.* The positions of leadership often increase the opportunities

and temptations to compromise this characteristic. The busy leader needs help, so how does he maintain a spirit of helpfulness toward others? In His discourse on the Good Shepherd, Jesus said, "The good shepherd lays down his life for the sheep" (John 10:11). Jesus expressed this most profoundly in the crucifixion, but He also demonstrated it in a daily way by His avoidance of privilege. Jesus gained nothing for himself by becoming our Savior and King.

Most leaders recognize that their role is one of sacrifice as they serve the Lord, and many work hard enough so that it is. But it is easy to slip into wanting a little compensation for that sacrifice. One can easily stay up to all hours of the night counseling and then get the feeling that he deserves a better bed; or sweats over a teaching for the people, and feel cheated if his car has no air conditioning; or carries the burden of guiding many souls and feels he shouldn't have to watch the children.

Jesus spoke to this clearly when He washed the feet of the disciples. "Do you know what I have done to you? You call me Teacher and Lord; and you are right, for so I am. If I then, your Lord and Teacher, have washed your feet you ought to wash one another's feet. For I have given you an example, that you also should do as I have done to you" (John 13:12-15). Jesus served in big ways as a Teacher, Healer, and Savior. And those were certainly sacrificial; they took His time, strength, and even His life. But for some reason He also chose to deny any privileges for His position, and He even found the most menial task and told us to follow Him in doing it. "Whoever would be great among you must be your servant, and whoever would be first among you must be slave of all. For the Son of man also came not to be served but to serve" (Mark 10:43-45).

What are the foot-washing services that a leader can do today to refresh his servant's perspective on life? That is a question which may need to be decided in each situation, but he should never think he is above any tasks. Leadership in servanthood does not have fringe benefits or privileges that others can't enjoy.

Home: the Proving Ground

We should not leave this discussion about the character of pastoral leaders without noting the parallel which Paul makes between how we function in our family and how we function in the church. "If a man does not know how to manage his own household, how can he care for God's church?" (1 Tim. 3:5). Leadership in the family is the closest approximation we have to leadership in the church. It is here, in the home situation, that we learn to be the kind of persons who are needed in the larger household of God. If we want to know what kind of leaders people will be in the church, we can see what kind of leaders they are in their own family settings.

The Family Connection

In our community, we have also found it helpful to know something about the families from which potential leaders have come. By now it has been amply demonstrated that the way we lead in our own families is largely determined (except for God's redemption) by the way our fathers and mothers conducted themselves during our childhood.

Someone who grew up with a lack of discipline in the home will have a difficult time exercising discipline in his own home. Someone who grew up with a stern and angry father will tend to be that kind of a father himself. A person who grew up in a home with weak leadership will likely be inclined toward a low level of leadership. On the other hand, people who have grown up with strong, loving parents who gave plenty of love and affection, but also set firm limits, have a base of experience that will greatly assist them in doing the same in their home and the church.

The carry-over from one generation to another may change in outward appearances but maintain an inner similarity. For instance, people who have grown up in a home without discipline may see what a disaster that was and decide they never want to repeat their parents' mistake. With this determination, they take a very diligent approach to discipline. But the fundamental insecurity which motivated the parents' lack of discipline may still be motivating the children's overly strict and rigid discipline.

These family patterns that pass from generation to generation do, of course, get redeemed and transformed by the power of Christ in homes where He is truly Lord. But the bad patterns of parents are not instantly removed. Normally, we must grow out of them over a period of years as the Spirit works a renewal of our minds (Rom. 12:2). Thus, an inquiry into the patterns of authority in our families of origin, and the degree of redemption that has happened if they were negative, can be useful in understanding our leadership potential.

Who Is Sufficient?

When we put all this together and reflect on what kind of person we are looking for in positions of pastoral leadership, we might be inclined to say, "Who is sufficient for these things?" The requirements are very high. There is no more exacting and difficult assignment in all the world, than that placed on someone who carries significant leadership responsibilities in the church.

And yet we can rejoice and have confidence, for it is the mighty power of God that is at work in us, as Paul so clearly expresses in 2 Corinthians 4. We are but earthen vessels, in whom and through whom the transcendent power and glory of the almighty God of heaven are being revealed in the world. So we do not lose heart. We have faith, we have Spirit! We speak with the same creative energy that was manifested when God first said, "Let light shine out of darkness."

The image of vessels is a good one, and Paul picks it up again in the pastoral epistles. "In a great house there are not only vessels of gold and silver but also of wood and earthenware, and some for noble use, some for ignoble. If anyone purifies himself from what is ignoble, then he will be a vessel for noble use, consecrated and useful to the master of the house, ready for any good work" (2 Tim. 2:20, 21). Let us cleanse ourselves from what is unclean, unworthy, and distracting, so that we may be "ready for any good work."

10

Men's and Women's Roles, a Split

There are few issues more volatile in the church and the world today than the differing attitudes about sex roles. Christian communities have not escaped the struggle. As a matter of sad fact, it is one of the major dividing issues between communities, even the networks of communities. Often when Jesus faced such a bind, He could point people to additional truth that freed them from the corners they were in.

The feminist controversy tends to break into two camps—traditionalists and egalitarians. Sterotypes seldom fit anyone, but some kind of a summation may be helpful in looking at the problem. The problem goes much deeper than quoting 1 Peter 3:1 ("wives, be submissive to your husbands") or Galatians 3:28 ("there is neither male nore female"). It has to do with the whole nature of the church.

The traditionalist sees a hierarchical order to society, and even the whole universe, in which each creature realizes its true meaning, freedom and wholeness by finding and fitting into its place. In terms of sex roles the traditionalist would say male supremacy is the norm in nature, and the Judeo-Christian tradition is patriarchal, not because God couldn't find a matriarchal or egalitarian culture through which to visit mankind, but by choice and design to reflect His own nature and intention for creation. To dismantle this order is not only to rebel against God's mysterious pattern, but to bring disastrous confusion down upon the heads of children who are still trying to establish their identity.

The traditionalist says that it is our technological society, which cares for nothing but production, which demands that if women can produce as well as men, then all role distinctions should end.

Not so, the egalitarian would respond. Liberation is not the product of technology but the product of the Gospel which offers to free everyone from his or her "place." The lofty picture of everyone joyfully finding his place in the beautiful tapestry of life, they say, is nothing but a tattered old rag that's been trotted out to justify feudalism, colonialism, slavery, racism, and male chauvinism. The egalitarian would point out that most traditionalists have acknowledged the error of their ways with regard to slavery and other such unjust relationships, and for the same reasons should accept correction on their antifeminist views. The egalitarians would also point out that their own views are not new but have their roots in the Reformation claim that each individual has the right to read the Scriptures for himself and come before God without any other intermediary than Christ. The fact that all people are sinners yet have access to the Father is such a leveling truth that any other distinctions are illegitimate. Through the years the egalitarian perspective was more fully developed through the evangelical or "low-church" traditions, which were, in fact, the major proponents of the abolition of slavery, the suffrage of women, and other human rights movements.

Problems with the Traditionalist View

The traditionalists' flag of a glorious hierarchy is indeed a tattered old rag, but that's not because it wasn't patterned after a finely woven vision. Its ideals capture some very important elements of God's order, but its disrepute comes from dragging that vision through the mud and using it as a mantle to cover and justify this world's systems. Since the appropriation of the church by Constantine for his own ends in the Fourth Century, the traditionalists have used the idea of a natural order to claim divine justification for systems that are quite contrary to Jesus' teachings. The solution is not to throw out the vision because it has been prostituted, but to redeem it for proper application. Even though there were times and places where some worldly systems may have seemed to coincide with a godly order, they usually failed on one or all of three counts. They were not voluntary. They permitted privilege. And the authorities were not submitted.

Problems with the Egalitarian View

It is not easy to be a reformer, and the egalitarian perspective is reformational in that it is in reaction to many very serious situations in the church. But the danger for the reformer is that in trying to remove the tumor, he may chop off the head. That's not far from what's happened in the egalitarians' operation on the body of Christ. Instead of the vision of headship, we are offered a utopia of opportunity. It usually increases justice by promoting voluntarism and reducing privilege, but it also becomes a bastion for individualists, isolationists and competitors. The egalitarian doesn't want to promote strife and jockeying for power, but if one's whole philosophy sees freedom as the securing of rights rather than finding one's place in God's order, the person creates an environment where one cannot risk disarmament and vulnerability. The most one can hope for is a keen eye to catch any imbalance of power.

In its most radical form egalitarianism just does not take into account the very pronounced theme of authority and submission that is found throughout the Scripture. Neither does it uphold the importance of the servant's heart and the biblical judgment on self-seeking, themes which in practice often clash with the securing of "rights."

Some modified egalitarians accept the need for leadership and authority within the body of Christ and confine their concerns to ensuring equal opportunity and eliminating prejudicial conditioning. But equal opportunity for what? At some point that view accepts the notion that certain roles are more privileged than others, and it spurs ambition to attain those positions. In the world that is true, and it has often been true in the church, but to accept and allow that to continue to be the case in the church is the same mistake that many traditionalists make.

11

Men's and Women's Roles, a Unity

Before we allow ourselves to drift into a polarization on the issue of men's and women's roles, aren't there some insights the Lord would like to show us that would draw us into unity? Each view outlined in the last chapter captures some truths and identifies other dangers, but how can we avoid a party spirit in which other brothers and sisters in Christ become our enemies? We *do* want Jesus to be Lord, and we want to fill out our Kingdom vision to include as much of God's ideal and justice as we can. We also know that Satan offers subtle perversions of that vision that seem to have merit but contain just enough error to subvert and discredit us. We don't want to be embarrassed to find we've been defending those deadly errors along with the truths. How can our view become a more perfect way, closer to the Kingdom vision?

The Kingdom vision truly is a vision of a kingdom rather than a democracy. We've grown up with a good deal of training and education about the merits of democracy and the glories of independence—the more the better. Even when we become disillusioned with our government, we usually contrast it with a better democracy, not a kingdom. And so we transfer those attitudes into our churches. We may talk about the "spiritual kingdom," but what we usually mean is the realm of the spirits—God, angels, Satan, demons, etc. We don't mean our church communities. When it gets down to people and what we do with our time from day to day, we want to preserve our independence through a kind of religious democracy that is somewhere between Robert's Rules of Order and do-your-own-thing. That is even true of churches which have an acknowledged hierarchical structure. In "ecclesiastical matters" the authority of the church may be accepted, but there are never louder complaints than when the church gives instruction in "personal matters," and often those complaints are not so much objections to the church's position as they are objections to the church's right to hold a position.

That's natural. It reflects who we are, and it reflects what we've been taught. We don't like to be told what to do, and as American we've learned to be very proud that no one *can* tell us what to do. But the Kingdom of God is a kingdom. Christ is the King who is ruler over all kings. That's His chosen form of government for His people.

Openness to Role Distinctions

Openness to role distinctions was a long time coming at Reba Place. Many of us had gone through quite an egalitarian stage. For some, their consciousness had not been raised to effect an homogenization of sex roles, but the basis for that was already laid in a somewhat political and historical suspicion of all authority. Our Anabaptist roots lent to that suspicion as did our involvement in the civil rights movement and the peace movement. For years the Fellowship got along without recognizing any elders. There were some strong leaders among us, but it was our style for them to keep as low a profile as possible. If you had to lead, you did it inconspicuously.

Our acceptance of the Baptism of the Holy Spirit some six years ago brought some correctives to this mind-set. We had never drifted into a do-your-own-thing approach, but had always recognized the authority of the body in our personal lives. All personal decisions were submitted to the body for testing. But it was an egalitarian body that we allowed to exist, somewhat as a check and balance to protect ourselves from "authority." Our acceptance of the Baptism of the Holy Spirit brought renewed study of the biblical imagery of the body of Christ, and we quickly had to admit that the Spirit is free to give various gifts to different people. We had no need to be jealous or fearful of those gifts, and therefore did not need to suppress them.

We began testing and affirming the gifts which were evident in our midst, and in so doing acknowledged some to be elders with gifts of leadership, teaching, counseling, etc. This new openness allowed the Lord to work far more freely in our midst. Problems that had lingered on for years began to get resolved. Growth ensued, and ministry that we thought was far beyond us began being worked through us by the power of the Spirit. It was only with this recognition of authority that we began ministering households. Before that time the collection of a number of people under one roof would have led to chaos, especially if some were very needy and troubled. In a way, we had kept the needy folks at a safe distance because we had no structure to deal with their needs.

Still it was some time before we looked at the question of men's and women's roles. We were accepting and benefiting from the functions of leadership in the church, but somewhere in the back of our minds we didn't see it as ideal. The need for leadership was thought of as a divinely ordained corrective necessary because of our immaturity. If we were all mature, we imagined that we wouldn't need any leaders. We'd just be a happy mob, all getting our directions transmitted to us through the air, straight from God.

But then we looked more closely at Jesus' relationship to the Father. No relationship perceived by man could be more ideal. It is the perfect relationship even though it didn't match our prejudices. Jesus and the Father are one in terms of worth, honor, power and glory. Jesus is not second-class divinity, but functionally Jesus is submitted to the Father in a way that the Father is not submitted to the Son. Functionally it is not reciprocal.

This understanding brought an openness in our

hearts to role distinctions that we'd not had before. They weren't defects for which we had to apologize. Role distinctions were part of God's plan for the family and the church. Our job was to seek God's will about how roles should be worked out so that they were God's best for everyone. We were very aware of how often "roles" have been abused in the name of God's order for things, so we knew there was a lot of danger, but we wanted to have the courage to face into that search without opting for the simple solution of eliminating roles.

Headship Begins in the Family

Ephesians 5:21-6:9 has often seemed to be a paradoxical passage in understanding men's and women's roles. Paul begins the passage by instructing us all to "be subject one to another." If one reads no further, Paul would seem to be teaching a mutual responsibility with no role distinctions in the church. But Paul then offers four examples. He first tells wives to submit to their husbands and husbands to love their wives. Did Paul just forget to remind husbands to also submit to their wives? Was he substituting the word "love" when he meant "submit" just so he could achieve literary variation? I don't think so. I believe that Paul was instructing us that everyone is to be submitted but not necessarily through a reciprocal submission.

The following examples make this meaning clear. The second example is of the church's submission to Christ. It's hard to imagine that Paul was suggesting that Christ is similarly subject to the church. The third is the submission of children to parents. Again the reverse is out of the question. We are responsible for our children and require their obedience. We do not let them ask for our obedience in the same way. And in his fourth example Paul instructs servants to submit to their masters. By definition the reverse is not envisioned. So, if husbands are not to be submitted to their wives in the same way that wives are to be submitted to them, are they exempt from submission?

Does Paul's opening phrase, "be subject one to another," not apply to them or Christ, parents and masters? No. The simplest understanding is that each person is to be submitted to another. Christ is subject to the Father as the church is subject to Christ. Husbands are to be *just as subject* to the church as wives are to be subject to their husbands, etc. Not reciprocal but real, from one to the next.

This and other passages led us to believe that God did have a plan for family headship which usually assigned the final responsibility to the man. It was not a matter of flipping a coin or a question for each couple to determine solely according to the apparent abilities of the partners. God did intend a pattern for the family which is reflected in His creation of the physical differences between men and women. Child bearing and initial nurturing are, of necessity, the woman's task. To accept the extension of that role is natural; to fight it is a contrivance.

Reba Place Fellowship is not dogmatic about the implications of this understanding when it comes to the church. However, the fact that the final responsibility for leadership in our church usually falls to men flows from our experience of the natural order in the family. In one sense the church is just a large, extended family; men are more practiced in leadership and usually more available for leadership. We are quite aware that that thinking may be unconvincing to anyone who is pushing a strong feminist view. But the Lord has led us in a quiet practice which seems to be personally freeing for both men and women. We accept the rightness of male headship in the family, and in oversight of the church. But within that context there is a lot of room for responsibility, use of gifts, and sharing of tasks.

As we were talking together about this chapter, my wife Neta said, "That's the mystery. It's a freedom I feel that I don't feel when I'm with groups who are crusading hard on either extreme. There's a basic context with lots of room to be God's children together. When I first came to Reba Place, my primary feeling was that I was taken seriously as a person, with gifts and needs, both of which the body seemed eager and willing to receive. There were challenges in learning deeper responsibilities of headship and submission—but it wasn't a crusade permeating every event or relationship."

One thing that the Fellowship did discover as it searched the Scriptures for God's perspective on the roles of men and women, was that even though the leadership of God's people was usually assigned to men, that was not true in every case. When God wanted to do so, He chose a woman. He was never hindered by a cultural bias (which may imply that the predominance of men was also not the product of a cultural bias). And we did not find any support for the theory that those women were God's "second choices" in the absence of willing men. From what we could see, God acts sovereignly to give gifts of leadership to whomever He chooses. Usually the final responsibility is placed in the hands of men, but He is the Giver to accomplish His purposes, and sometimes He chooses a woman.

Though the final responsibility of leadership in our community is usually carried by men, there are many other very important leadership tasks that women fulfill. They lead several ministries: the dance group, the music group, the hospitality ministry, Christian education for the children, the day-care center, etc. Our household managers are currently all women. They carry out the coordination of most of the daily functions in the house. They work with the elder in the household who has the broader pastoral oversight for the group. Usually the elder and household manager are a husband and wife team. Most of our households include one or more other persons, either men or women, in the leadership team to help provide objectivity in the group. Our elders circle includes two women; one is also the head of a household, and the circle has included other women in the past. There are three senior elders, at this time all men. Though, if God should call a woman to this position, we would need to be open to that possibility.

Correctives for the Family and Church

Through our experience we have discovered a number of important principles for helping us live more smoothly with the order that the Lord brings into our lives. Many of the things that we have learned about men's and women's roles in the family and church reiterate what has already been covered in the chapters dealing with general authority, submission and free will, but it is valuable to review them again as they apply specifically to men's and women's roles.

1. *There are to be no special privileges for men.* We deeply believe that God does not respect one person more than another, and the role He gives each person in the body in no way reflects that person's worth. By one spirit we were baptized into one body—Jews or Gentiles, males or females, slaves or free. Paul teaches in 1 Corinthians 12 that there is to be no jealousy or competition between the distinct parts of the body because they are each of equal worth, deserving equal care. Because there is plenty of love, acceptance and blessing to go around, it makes no difference whether God asks certain individuals to take one role and others another. In fact, it doesn't make any difference if He asks whole groups to do one task, even if that group is distinct sexually. It is only by permitting the notion or practice of privilege for some and shortage for others that we give substance to the struggle over roles.

In the most elementary way that equality of love and care is symbolized in our community by the practice of the common purse. All members receive an equal allowance unless there is some special expense that they have to meet which has been approved by the body.

This attitude of no privilege for persons in authority is so contrary to the world's notion that we must be careful that our old practices do not subtly find their way into the Kingdom life. The husband who kicks off his shoes and sits down in the easy chair after dinner to read the paper while he expects his wife to clean up the dishes, put the kids to bed and do the mending for the next two hours may be operating from an old attitude of personal privilege. He may be presuming that his job for eight hours is more important than the work his wife does for fourteen. If she had rested for half the afternoon, it might be okay for him to take his turn in the evening. But otherwise the expectation of such privilege and the attitude of self importance is an old worldly view that pollutes our Kingdom and cannot be encouaged.

2. *Authority means sacrifice, love and responsibility.* Jesus did not renounce His authority, but He offered us an example of the Kingdom the way it is to be exercised. It is first of all sacrificial servanthood. In laying down His life for us in obedience to the Father, Jesus' authority was manifested. That sacrifice enhanced His headship over the church and is what enables us to follow Him. That kind of sacrifice is what true authority is. Sacrifice is in direct contrast to the privilege that the world equates with authority. Sacrificial leadership means going first and farthest through difficult trials, not driving or even urging others ahead of you.

In certain situations sacrificial headship means accepting unilateral blame for a mistake to which others have contributed. I've found this one of the most difficult aspects of leadership. My ego resists and wants to make sure everyone understands all the extenuating circumstances and accepts his share of the responsibility as I admit to mine. Jesus, however, went to the cross and fully accepted the unjust punishment for our sins. Most of us have yet to understand our responsibility fully. The sacrificial leader must follow Jesus in that role when it is needed to bring reconciliation. Bringing others to an understanding of their own responsibility should be done only for their own good and maturity and not the leader's vindication.

Ephesians 5 charges husbands to love their wives as Christ loves the church and gave himself for it. Frequently when couples are struggling with the issue of authority and submission in their marriage, the discussion gets derailed over the wife's difficulty with submitting. And that's no small issue; the wife may have had a long-standing authority conflict or some very bad experiences that have eroded her trust from childhood on, but the *idea* of submitting is not very elusive. Whether we like it or not, we can usually comprehend it. Men, on the other hand, are faced with an assignment that is hard to fully comprehend. They are told to love like Christ loves. Paul enumerates the details of that kind of love in 1 Corinthians 13: Love is patient and kind; it is not jealous or boastful, arrogant or rude, irritable or resentful. It does not insist on its own way. It does not rejoice in wrong but in right. Love bears all things, believes all things, hopes all things, endures all things. And it never ends.

A wife cannot excuse her lack of submission by her husband's lack of love, and a husband cannot excuse his lack of love by his wife's rebellion. But most wives are more easily able to take steps of faith in the area of submission if they know that their husbands are asking the Lord to help them develop Christ's kind of love.

Headship is finally responsibility. Our concepts of the roles of leadership are often too simple. We often reduce the roles to the most obvious task stereotypes. And frequently these stereotypes have been created by the world and not God's Word. For instance, a man's headship in his family is not made or destroyed on whether he does domestic chores or not. And a woman's submission is not determined by whether she avoids certain out-front activities which represent the family. The issue of submission and authority may be determined by *why* the individual does or does not do those things, but not by the superficial tasks themselves. In some situations where people's roles are very insecure there may be some effort to resort to superficial task distinctions as a way to give the illusion of proper structure, but that can be a ruse. We all know of families where there are sharply separated tasks between the husband and wife without the husband being in any way the true head of the family. Headship comes by reason of accepted responsibility. Once that's clear, you can delegate any task or help with any task. I have never become the mother in our family because I change diapers and take my turn at dishes. I have always remained the father, the man sharing those tasks.

Learning that headship is not a superficial task separation, but a deepening involvement with and responsibility for my family, has helped me participate more in my children's lives. I have found it to be a great privilege to actively care for our children while they are young. I wouldn't trade a thousand fishing trips for the nights that I've bathed our kids, rocked them while I read a story, prayed with them and then tucked them in bed. It's an experience I'll never get again with them. I've had to learn a lot of patience, firmness and love that briefer contacts would not have demanded. Those lessons are useful elsewhere as I try to be a good pastor. The Lord is using them to teach me to be the kind of person I want to become.

As for our children, the way they experience me will provide their first understandings of the character of God our Father. I won't manage to be perfect, but I hope they won't have too many memories to heal or misconceptions to change. I don't want them to think of God as distant, cold, unapproachable or unconcerned about their little needs. I hope they will sense in their deepest being that they can always come to our Father in heaven, that He'll have time for them to crawl up into His lap and be cared for. I also want them to know that God is in charge, will protect them and cannot be manipulated. But at an early age, availability and tenderness is very important. If I were a hardliner on task distinctions, I might inadvertently miss out on a lot of that time with the kids.

3. *Submission must be voluntary.* Christian marriage, like all other adult Kingdom relationships, is voluntary. God has designed the ideal structure for that relationship, but no one is forced to enter that relationship.

It does not seem to me that single women in the community are under a scriptural injunction to be any more explicitly submitted than men or that they need to find some *man* whose "care" they can be under. We all should be accountable to a pastor in a very real way, and in a church where the final responsibility is in the hands of men that may mean that single women are finally accountable to leaders who happen to be men, but their personal pastor or counselor could easily be another woman. And their tasks and ministry in the church can range far and wide and might include responsibility for men.

Marriage seems to be the only one-to-one relationship where God expects the man to definitely be the head, and entrance into marriage is voluntary. It is important for both men and women to consider this before marriage. If the relationship is to exist in a biblical manner, then it needs to follow God's pattern. One should not enter it calling it "Christian" if it is built on some other model.

If a person has already entered marriage and is attempting to make it biblical, that too is something that cannot be forced. The husband can teach and invite, but he should not force. His primary agenda is to love, serve and accept responsibility for the family. If the wife is not ready to submit, it is good to remember that Christ loved the church and gave himself for her long before she submitted, "while we were yet in sin." If the husband did not win his wife's submission before marriage, then he needs to go back and complete his courting process. He is still responsible.

It is good to look a little more closely at the importance of voluntarism and the elimination of privilege. As was noted earlier, many worldly systems tried to justify their existence by the Kingdom vision. We need to admit that the church acquiesced in that prostitution of its approval. We need to clearly see why the worldly systems were not true parts of the Kingdom. Take the issue of slavery, for instance. Its evil is not in the fact that one man is serving another man and is under his authority. But its evil is in the fact that it is an involuntary relationship in which the served realizes privileges denied the servant. Paul's letter to Philemon illustrates this clearly. Onesimus, a runaway slave belonging to Philemon, was converted through Paul's witness. Paul does not recommend the termination of the servant relationship, but attempts to re-establish it on a Kingdom basis. He sends Onesimus back to Philemon, not under arrest or under guard, but as the bearer of his own letter of reference. Certainly Onesimus made a free choice to return before he left Paul and had many opportunities on the trip to reconsider that decision. Also Paul requested, even insisted, that Philemon receive Onesimus as a *brother* and not as a slave. That establishes the issue of worth, but it did not change Onesimus' role as a servant. Paul had enjoyed and even coveted his service, and Paul was expecting Onesimus to be an even better servant now that he was a Christian. But the brotherly reception that Paul insisted upon would have completely ruled out Philemon's realizing privileges at Onesimus' expense.

Our integrity in promoting a Kingdom vision which includes differences in roles must acknowledge some of the past errors of the church. Otherwise those who have identified injustices have reason to fear that they will be repeated.

4. *Submission must not be purchased by tokenism.* Another distinction between the Kingdom vision and worldly patterns is in the practice of purchased submission. In ancient warfare when a besieged king sued for peace, he often tried to negotiate for as much autonomy as possible. Sometimes all that the invaders wanted was an agreement to an annual tax and the promise of no rebellion. Then they'd pack up their war machines and move on to new conquests.

Sometimes the conflict over men's and women's roles is settled in a similar way. Men agree to give women certain areas of token autonomy so that both the men and women can have a sense of worth and accomplishment. In exchange the women agree to let the men do certain things without interference. That's an unresolved conflict! And any sense of worth coming out of it is not Kingdom worth. When Jesus asks to be Lord of our lives, we don't negotiate for private autonomy in the kitchen. If we do, we've missed the whole point and have actually agreed to a very poor bargain. If our meaning and worth is to come from exercising autonomy, then we might as well exercise it over as much area as we can manage. If, on the other hand, we've caught the vision of the worth and meaning of being a child of God and a partaker of His life in His Kingdom (rather than having a little one of our own), it is obviously better to sell all for the pearl of great price.

Such an unresolved conflict can also lead to a very subtle pattern of manipulation. It is sometimes expressed in a sickening, feigned submission in which the wife has learned to dote on her husband in certain ways which build up his ego, thereby purchasing her autonomy and even control of the family. In its most extreme form, sex itself is used as a carrot-stick tool to achieve a happy family or pacify the husband. Even when these techniques are not used to control, they often cause the wife to aspire to become an empty-headed, private floozy that falls very short of the biblical image of womanhood and is no compliment to any man who will accept such a demeaning role for his wife.

5. *Responsible submission is necessary.* The biblical image of womanhood is probably nowhere expressed so fully as in Proverbs 31. The woman in that passage is valued far more than rubies, not because she is tinsel for her husband's ego, but because she is a widely respected, strong woman who is able to wisely manage the entire household, make good business decisions, and plan for the future. She is not the head of the family, but she is her husband's trusted and totally capable representative. She is said to "open her mouth with wisdom," and her husband would be an insecure fool not to seek and accept it.

If our meaning and worth in life is not to be achieved with the Lord by carving out an area of autonomy where we can enjoy the illusion of accomplishment, where is our meaning? We are "heirs and joint heirs with Christ" of His whole Kingdom. "All these things shall be added unto us." We are very responsible participants in the whole. The fact that headship means final responsibility does not relieve others of the need for responsible submission.

The authority that Christ has given His church while remaining head over the church demonstrates this. In terms of role relationships within the church or within the family this is also true. Each person in submission is responsible to test, evaluate, and pray about the recommendations from the leaders. If a wife cannot affirm a direction that her husband suggests for the family, she'd better not rubber-stamp it. She is responsible to humbly share her questions and reservations. And he's responsible to humbly receive those in a very serious way, and if they cannot come to some resolution between themselves, he's smart if he shares it with someone else for outside counsel.

In our Fellowship many mistakes of the elders have been caught and corrected by other members who, in a spirit of unity, shared their reservations and concerns. This must also happen in our families; it is the kind of wisdom and spiritual maturity that the woman of Proverbs 31 contributes. The goal in the church and family is unity, not wooden headship and blind obedience.

6. *All heads are to be submitted.* If wives are not to wring their meaning in the Kingdom from some token autonomy in the kitchen, then husbands are not to look for their meaning in making their families and homes little fiefs. Our meaning comes from being children of God and having a place in the Kingdom. We reject the notion on every level that the *nature* of our place or role is the source of our meaning. We should all be ready and grateful to accept any position, believing that one is as blessed as another.

Actually, any man who asks his wife to submit to his headship while himself refusing to submit *as literally* to the authority of the church (as administered through real people like himself) is a pretender and usurper to the lordship of Christ. This is because, if the whole understanding of the Kingdom and submission and authority has any validity, then it is only as a channel for being submitted to the Lord. Whenever we cap off that channel, we have a reproduction of Adam's rebellion when he decided that he was going to handle the situation himself rather than submit to God. All godly authority proceeds from submission. All other authority is antichrist in nature.

This call for all Christians to live in submission removes the sense of injustice from asking wives to submit to husbands who don't have to submit to anybody. This is another way that the Kingdom vision differs importantly from the world's system. When the worldly view of a man's home being his castle insulates him from submission to the church, he has missed the Kingdom vision. The family is not the basic unit through which God relates to mankind. The church is God's basic unit. It is the body of Christ.

In summary, our role in God's Kingdom is made precious, not by reason of its importance in worldly standards which build or insult our egos, but by reason of our relationship to Jesus and the fact that we have a place in His Kingdom at all. When we think of how great God is, the distinctions between our roles become insignificant. We have no cause to lord our position over one person or scramble to rise above another. Our whole attention should be focused on affirming one another as chosen children of the Father who have been given worthy and honorable tasks in the Kingdom, regardless of their comparative worldly greatness.

"For the body does not consist of one member but of many.... God arranged the organs in the body, each one of them, as he chose.... The parts of the body which seem to be weaker are indispensable.... And so God has composed the body to give greater honor to the inferior parts, that there may be no discord in the body, but that the members may have the same care for one another" (1 Cor. 12:14-25).

Part Three

Personal Implications

12

Aid for the Walking Wounded

Life in a solid Christian community often uncovers
some perturbing things. We find that the Lord's army
is made up of many "walking wounded"—folks who
have needed healing of some sort for a long time, but
have never been in a place where they could have received it. So they kept on going, coping with their pain
the best way they could.

That's not good. The Gospel of Christ offers salvation for the whole man: "Come to me, all who labor
and are heavy laden, . . . and you will find rest for
your souls. For my yoke is easy, and my burden is
light" (Matt. 11:28). To neglect the healing for the
individual is as serious as overlooking the brokenness
in the body at large. Both reduce our integrity and
limit the abundant life. It is the height of arrogance
to limp right past Jesus' offer of healing and think
we can go out and proclaim that He is Lord. Yet it
is easy to do. We even shy away from picking up the
burdens of others. Sometimes we don't know how, but
too often the admission of such widespread need in
the church shines too much light on ourselves, and
we'd just rather not take a look.

This head-in-the-sand policy is so widespread among
many Christians that they are often surprised when
they see a formerly very active Christian enter community, cut back on much of his ministry and responsibility and begin having "personal struggles." Why?
Does the community create problems that were never
there before?

I do not think so. Our experience has been that it is the *safe environment* that uncovers problems too threatening to deal with elsewhere. In the person's more solitary past he may have repressed feelings that frightened him because he might lose control or be rejected. Or he may have ignored problems thinking that there was no solution. Many folks appear to be coping while the pressure builds all the time. Others find respectable outlets that give them a sense of relief while hiding the problem. Some drown themselves in their work; others move to a new location, or change jobs or churches or get a divorce, etc. But in the community for the first time they may feel safe enough to face the source. Sometimes that is accompanied with a behavioral let-down, a dropping of the pretense of coping.

Some of the more frequent wounds that people are walking around with are the inability to cope with feelings, insecurity in God's love, subliminal fears of an impending emotional breakdown, shaky marriages, guilt over serious unconfessed sins, on-going sinful conditions, resentment that saps one's energy or causes the person to fear vulnerability, separation and grief that were never fully processed.

A couple of examples might be useful. When Pam and her husband came into the community a little over three years ago, they were comparatively new Christians. Their friends thought that they were being very noble to dedicate their lives to God in this way. They had known Pam and her husband as an exciting, friendly couple who seemed to be very well adjusted. No one believed that they had any troubles, at least none that they couldn't handle themselves. Pam was very civic-minded, an ideal, modern mother who took her daughters for long walks in the woods to observe the wildlife. Her husband was a respected and liked English teacher in the local junior high school.

They may have lived as if they had the world by the tail, but underneath it was different. Their marriage was falling apart. Pam was relating to her husband and children as though she were a child, manipulating them to fill her emotional needs. And having never dealt with her feelings, her needs were great—stored up over the years from such experiences as feeling parental rejection and having an illegal abortion. Pam had come from a well-educated, success-oriented family where emotional problems had been the norm—everybody had them and one just hoped that he could keep the lid on and not end up in a mental hospital. So Pam stuffed her feelings down and coped as well as she could.

Her husband wasn't doing much better. He was an emotional sponge himself, spoiled by a childhood of over-indulgence and self-serving. He didn't know how to give to anybody, let alone how to take control and give to his needy wife and children. He was drinking too much. His teaching career *actually* wasn't going well at all. He was seeing a psychiatrist and taking tranquilizers just to get through the day.

But none of this was obvious to their friends in the small town where they lived. To their friends, Pam and her husband were heading off to serve others in their own idealistic way.

After coming to community, Pam's husband took leave of his teaching career and accepted a job as a gardener. Gradually he began to devote more and more attention to learning how to give to his family and lead them.

At first Pam was shocked to see people who were whole in spirit. She thought that the even and happy emotions that the people around her expressed were phony. When she and her husband later moved into a household, she couldn't believe that marriage could be as stable as she observed it to be in the leadership couple. It was solid, honest, and not filled with unresolved fights.

Pam recalls that she became aware of deep problems that she had not acknowledged in her life until after coming to community, and she began to experience the pain that had been stored up inside her for years. That emotional pain was so acute that she experienced it as a physical pain in her stomach for months. Also, in counseling with her elder she would confess overwhelming fear—cold panic. But she didn't know what she feared. The pain was so great that she didn't feel as though she had any control of herself any longer. Slowly she began to be able to see that the fear came from feeling out of control, and that she felt out of control because of the flood of pain that was finally finding its way out.

"I was actually afraid," she reports, "that if I let go, I would most certainly go insane, and then I would die, physically die. During my whole life that's what I saw happen to people around me. I thought that if a person didn't hold himself together for all he was worth, he'd fall apart and go insane, from which there was no real recovery.

"Finally with the help of my elder and small group I was able to realize that the source of that fear was Satan. He was the one who wanted to destroy me, and I was no match for him if I continued trying to do it on my own. But the good news was that Jesus is stronger than Satan. As I began to be able to claim that in faith, I began to get release from the panic. Jesus was not going to let Satan destroy me. Even if I fell apart, I was safe in His arms and in the midst of these brothers and sisters."

Again and again the Lord reassured Pam that if she fell apart, He was still going to love and take care of her. Isaiah 43 became very meaningful where it says, "When you pass through the waters, I will be with you; and through the rivers, they shall not overwhelm you; when you walk through the fire, you shall not be burned, and the flame shall not consume you."

"The Lord showed me that I *did* have to go through the fire to purge out all that rotten stuff in me," says Pam. "But He promised me that I would not be burned. It was so hard to give up that protection of myself. It was all I'd ever known, but the Lord wanted me to throw myself completely on Him. Time and again I'd get very rebellious and say that I was not going to surrender, but I knew that if I didn't let the Lord take me through the fire, I would explode on my own. There was too much stuff in me that needed healing.

"Slowly the sense of the Lord's care in the midst of the body began to replace the pain. I had visions of sitting on God the Father's lap, being rocked like a little child. I could cry and let the pain come out, but there was also the love and joy that was growing within.

"Now for me, the most wonderful part is the sound mind. The fear of having a wounded mind that might someday fall apart goes back through my whole life, and the freedom from that fear is as though everything within me has been made new. The Lord's cleaned it all out and filled me with himself. There's a great sense of strength within me, and I know that it is the Lord. The panic has been gone now for a long time, and I no longer even have periods of depression."

Pam is convinced that she could have never experienced the healing she's received if she had remained in an isolated setting. She sees the care that the body gave her as one of God's objectives for His church. "I know that the Lord can do anything. Even if I'd fallen apart out on my own, I know now that the Lord's love would have been as real, but could I have received it? I wouldn't recommend anyone trying that. Christ had a good reason for establishing His church. The people in it are the communicators of God's love and security, the environment in which we realize His presence. To anyone who's still on his own, I'd recommend simply turning to the Lord. A person wouldn't try to perform a physical operation on himself, and he shouldn't try a spiritual one alone either. Let the Lord use the instruments He set up. Let Him work through His body."

Another example of a walking wounded Christian was Rod. Rod held a national position with a major Christian organization yet he was not being pastored and supported. Both in the Christian organization for which Rod worked and in his church fellowship, no one monitored Rod's personal life and growth. In the former, spirituality was measured in terms of productivity. In the latter, there was not the pastoral authority

that Rod needed. He was very productive, so he was
seen by most as a gifted, spiritual, young man with a
lot of drive and a promising career before him—serving
the Lord. He had a pleasant home, a dynamic wife
(which was a feather in his cap at the organization),
and green lights all around. For four years he rose
steadily in the organization. Oh, he knew that there were
some problems in his life. He realized, for instance,
that he struggled with lust a lot. Occasionally he hinted
at the problem with his associates. They prayed with
him sometimes or joked self-consciously and said that
everyone had to tolerate a certain duality within one's
self; "After all, none of us are perfect." By their standards the Lord did seem to be counterbalancing his
impurity—productivity was continuing. God was blessing. All seemed well.

Then Rod discovered that his wife had had an affair.
He recalls that as he heard the news, the words that
kept going through his mind were, "I'm dead. I'm dead.
And all that I've ever been or tried to be is dead."

In order to hold the marriage together Rod and his
wife sought the help of a charismatic community with
strong pastoral gifts. There he hoped for some help in
putting his family back together, but he came with little
understanding of what had blown it apart.

Slowly Rod began to hear the ways that he had contributed to the problem in the family; he even came
to see that he carried the primary responsibility. "I
think that I was aware of some of the needs all along,"
said Rod. "But I felt so comfortable in my arena of
production that I could ignore the severity of need elsewhere. My wife and family were unattended by me.
Oh, I was around, except when I was away on trips,
but I wasn't taking responsibility. I closed my eyes to
the fact that my wife was getting fed up with that kind
of a relationship. She was angry, confused and hurting,
and I couldn't see that. I thought things were fine.

"Because the leadership gifts that I had were not
under pastoral direction, they became my way of developing an identity. At the only point that I was being
monitored (my production), I was doing fine, and

I was proud of it. My self-image got grandiose, and a lot of garbage went unnoticed. In particular I was tolerating this sexual fantasy business year after year. I struggled with it and I knew that my lust wasn't pleasing to the Lord, yet I'd come to accept it out of resignation.

"By accepting that duality in myself, I came to accept duality in other people, particularly my family. I learned to live with several conditions that weren't right, any one of which could have blown up.

"Finally, I came to realize that my identity, in fact my entire spiritual health, did not depend upon my job performance abilities."

Rod's thinking had been backwards for so many years that to get it reoriented and to keep his priorities straight, he quit his job and virtually dropped out of sight from the national Christian scene for two years. He took a low-level job as a clerical worker in a secular business (where he couldn't pretend at spirituality via ministry) and focused on his family and his personal integrity. Time and again he had to be recalled from the temptation to think that the community didn't understand him or appreciate his gifts. It was easy for him to offer himself as the solution to the problems he saw around him.

But now he's grateful for having been brought fully to the cross. "What the Lord was doing was bringing my life down to ground zero so that He could rebuild it on a solid foundation. Few people my age with a family have that luxury of taking time out to get their house in order. Actually, it is surprising. I found that the lust problem was an effect, not the cause. It disappeared when I really came under the submission to a spiritual pastor. Some of the other things, like my prideful outlook on life that had gotten me in so much trouble, took a little longer. I really wish someone could have blown the whistle on me earlier so that we wouldn't have had to go through so much pain. But then I don't know who could have done it. We weren't involved in a church life where that was happening."

Rod is now back into full-time ministry together with

his wife, both within and without the community. But his life is known and shared. He gets challenged when he gets carried away with his own importance or gets his priorities mixed up. His gifts were not falsely discerned. He's quite as capable as people used to think he was, but his energies are pulling evenly now.

Not everyone limps into community, but most of us have come with some substantial needs of one sort or another that weren't being met elsewhere. To keep a church healthy, problems must be uncovered and faced, and that can best happen in a life together.

I have a good Christian friend who doesn't live in community. He is very much impressed by the story of Corrie ten Boom and how her faith survived in a Nazi prison camp. "What will you do," he asked, "if your community is ever driven apart by persecution or something? Shouldn't you learn how to live successfully on your own so that you don't have to rely so much on each other?"

I don't think that persecution is something you can practice for by being alone. In fact, should the Lord ever call upon us to witness for Him in a solitary way, one of our greatest strengths will be the knowledge that even though we've been ripped apart we belong together. To know that you *do* belong, are remembered and prayed for by brothers and sisters offers great support.

Having a base of security and accountability where a person is supported, tested for integrity and strengthened will always result in stronger ministry. Community should not be a place where one gets lost in introspection, but it should be a solid foundation for outreach.

13

Take a Sounding (Counseling)

A few years ago in a small, New England church one of the elders felt burdened to open his home to share the life of Christ on a daily basis. He hardly knew the word "community," as he put it, but the Lord had done a lot for him and his wife, and now that their children were grown and gone they wanted to share their home with others. They opened their doors to several needy people, many of them were new Christians right off the street. Soon problems started developing, not only because the close life together brought things to the light that otherwise might have been overlooked, but the love that the people experienced in the household caused them to feel safe enough to want to deal with their problems.

The elder who was the head of the household didn't quite know what to do, so he went to the minister and the other elders for their support and help. But to that point they had had very little experience in a counseling ministry and basically didn't feel that all the heavy stuff was necessary. The minister led in this opinion partially because he had some deep needs in his own life that he didn't want to deal with and partially because he felt that if he would acknowledge his own inadequacy, it would undermine his authority and threaten his ministry. He said that he was in favor of community and even wanted to start a couple more households, but he wanted them to be primarily for fellowship and the economic and practical benefits of living together.

Needless to say, that left the already established household and its elder in real trouble. They all knew something about the depth of their need. Were they going to forget that it existed simply because the minister wanted to run shallow? They were past the point where they could turn back, and they could hardly wait until the other households had operated long enough to again press the issue of depth. What were they to do?

The problem is not unique, it occurs over and over again as new communities struggle with, sometimes resist, and sometimes accept the depth of human need to which the body of Christ must minister. We'd all like to solve our problems with a prayer or an admonition, but it is not that easy. We need to take a sounding. We need to know our limitations. And we need to know when we must go for help.

A healthy environment centered on the praise of the Lord Jesus Christ can be one of the most healing things in a person's life if it includes an open and honest accountability to the body, wise and insightful counsel, shared decision making to avoid foolish mistakes outside God's will, and a dedication to service and sacrifice. These points have been emphasized elsewhere in this book.

But there are times when more depth is needed. Formal secular training is often valuable. Reba Place sent Conrad Wetzel to graduate school to get a Ph.D. in psychology under the guidance of Hobart Mowrer at the University of Illinois. John Miller, one of the founders of the Fellowship, became the head of the Rehabilitation Department at Chicago State Hospital. Others acquired further training and professional experience. In fact, at one point as many as ten people would pile into a van and drive off to work at Chicago State every day. John Lehman's years of work as a social worker with the Juvenile Protection Agency has broadened his background. Recently, Jim and Charlotte Stringham, a psychiatrist and psychiatric nurse, moved to the Fellowship and have become members. They are now sharing with us their 20 years of experience.

We've found this knowledge to be very useful even

though secular theories about the human personality must always be tested with the Bible. Deep counseling is soul surgery. It deals with people's lives just as certainly as a scalpel. We don't expect a med student to practice medicine alone. Neither should young people go off on their own and think that they can start a community and take pastoral responsibility for others without having first done their homework, internship and residency in an already established community with counseling experience.

In our search for helpful tools in healing, Russ Harris, one of our members who received his Ph.D. from Michigan State University, applied his training in adult education and behavorial therapy to develop a system of charts to help us in the "renewal of the mind." The renewal of our minds is accomplished in many ways, but these charts help diagram one's choices in a practical way. In one of their simplest forms they were able to help a person like Ernie.

Ernie and his family came to the Fellowship with some serious problems, one of which was that he would periodically take a paycheck and run away—leave town for several days, often going south to his relatives in Alabama. Within a week or so he would phone his wife to report that he was broke and repentant and wanted to come home. Could she borrow and wire him the bus fare? This happened a dozen times before they came to the Fellowship and didn't automatically stop because they arrived at Reba. It was almost more than his wife could take and was doing noticeable damage to the children.

Along with some fairly comprehensive help for family management to relieve some of the pressures that would overwhelm Ernie, we created a chart called, "Twelve Decisions You Must Make Before You Can Reach Alabama." The chart included points like refusing to share his problems, choosing a plan to run, getting on the bus, not getting off the bus at various stops, etc. This was to help Ernie realize that just because the idea came into his head to escape his problems, he needn't feel it was inevitable that the whole painful event run its course. After making the chart, which Ernie kept in his billfold at all times, he only left once for as long as the family remained in the community. And then he was able to interrupt the sequence before he got on the bus to Alabama. He took the "special escape option" noted on the chart of checking into a hotel before leaving town to think about what he was doing. He phoned home to ask for prayer and say that he'd been gone all afternoon eating a big steak dinner and sitting through a couple movies. He guessed he really didn't want to run and would be home in an hour.

Far more complete charts catalogue several stimuli that often give the person problems and then detail the various steps and choices involved in realizing Kingdom behavior over old perceptions, old feelings, and old behavior. There are also ways to trace back from the behavior to its stimuli and recover if a person makes a wrong choice along the way.

As well as helping a person to make choices and be freed from old patterns, we have found charts useful in consolidating the healing that comes through other means. Often when a person is delivered from a problem through prayer or wise and insightful counsel, the healing doesn't last. That does not mean it wasn't genuine. The bonds of a problem may be truly broken at one point, yet the person can slip back into the problem as a habit.

Charts can be useful in these situations simply by providing the person with a reminder through regular monitoring and accountability. For this, a different kind of chart is sometimes useful. It can be designed like a graph or score card to encourage the person as he observes the freedom the Lord has given.

Healing of Memories

Loosening a person from the grip of the past through the "healing of memories" is one approach that has given us breakthroughs with problems that didn't seem to respond to the benefits of disciplined living, insightful counseling or prayers of deliverance. Through the contributions of John Bedford, a Baptist pastor from a community in England, our approach to the healing of memories was greatly expanded beyond the more hasty practices prominent in the States. We do not try to compress a person's lifetime of experiences into a four-to-eight-hour session of interviews and prayer. Instead, we allow enough time to be thorough, or we return to the subject over a period of weeks.

To become more familiar with how to help people experience healing of memories and to get an idea of what that could and could not do in a person's life, most of the elders personally underwent a series of sessions. Then we were ready to share our findings with other folks in the body.

Gail was one of those. As she shared her story, it became apparent that two things characterized her life experience. She had always felt insecure and afraid in spite of a number of remarkably independent ventures—ventures she had been driven to by a need to earn people's approval through high performance.

Further investigation showed that Gail had grown up in a home with a very unhappy, moody mother who had no reservoir of love to pass along to her daughters. She cared for them physically but resented her boring life and despised her husband for his lack of education. He got back at her by insulting her. Gail's mother never seemed to have any friends; she was aloof, businesslike, and well educated. She revealed her feelings only when she complained. Gail began to feel responsible for the poor marriage and felt she should somehow save her mother.

Finally, she discovered that she could make her mother happy through her accomplishments. (In retrospect, her accomplishments seem to have been a vicarious escape for her mother.) So Gail did well in school, drama, social graces, and other things, but she never felt that she deserved the various awards, honors or grades she received. That was partially because her efforts to bring peace to her mother brought no true security for herself. Also Gail was disturbed because she was developing an incredible loathing for her mother that would erupt in calling her names, mocking her, and even trying to hurt her physically. The guilt from that behavior, of course, fed into the vicious cycle of unworthiness, insecurity and fear.

Throughout her adult life, Gail's need to achieve continued to drive her to many accomplishments, but it also drove her frantic because it did not achieve security. She went through a number of relationships with men, sometimes using them, sometimes looking for love, sometimes both. She tried various forms of therapy; the insights focused her anger toward her family so that she cut off all communications with them at one point, but she didn't feel better. She studied Zen in a monastery in Japan for six months, got involved in a number of radical political causes, and even went to Cuba to cut sugar cane. She taught school, got into women's lib, and married a man on his urging to help him care for his children by a previous marriage. But the marriage broke down. Each change was one more option that didn't work out.

After Gail came to Reba Place, she met the Lord and her whole life began to change. But there was a core of insecurity that haunted her. Even after we patiently went through her whole life, dealing with the guilts and resentments that had accumulated from all those situations, there was still a weight of pain from which she wanted release. An important breakthrough came during a prayer in which the Lord allowed Gail to envision herself as an infant sitting on a rug in her dreary house. Outside it seemed bright and sunny, but inside it was cold and hard. Behind her stood Jesus. Across the room her mother was working with her back to her, completely unresponsive to Gail's every effort to cry out or attract her attention. As the pain of rejection mounted, Gail's feelings oscillated between a great hunger for her mother's attention and frustration that she wouldn't turn around. Finally as we waited, Gail cried out that she couldn't stand being alone any more. She begged Jesus to cause her mother to come to her and love her.

As we prayed, we felt led to speak for Jesus and say that her mother would not come. That was a fact of her life, and she needed to accept the pain of it rather than run from that pain as she had always done. But it seemed too much. No baby could tolerate that pain. She was sure it would utterly annihilate her.

Again we spoke for Jesus, "That is the pain that I faced, Gail, being forsaken by my Father in heaven. Do not shrink from the cup that is before you."

"But isn't there some other way?"

"No. He who loves his life will lose it, as you have found out. But he who would serve me must follow me."

Her sobs rose and shook her for a long time, then slowly subsided in acceptance.

"Gail, are you there?" we asked in Jesus' stead.

"Yes."

"How are you?"

"Just empty."

"Then turn around, Gail."

Then the realization struck her. Jesus had been there with her through the whole experience. She had not only survived the very pain that she had feared most, but in not running she had found that Jesus was with her through it all.

Struggles were not over for Gail, but she had found a new way to understand her childhood. It took time to integrate her insightful experiences into true healing. When the compulsion to drive herself now arises or the fear of abandonment haunts her, others in the body can remind her of the way the Lord went with her through that most painful point in her past and will be with her again. Death has lost its sting; Jesus has gone with her to taste it.

It is important to realize how much our past experiences can grip and mold us. Counseling with folks like Gail takes one deeper than the more popular forms of healing of memories. In the last few years we have become acquainted with Frank Lake, a charismatic Christian psychiatrist in England who runs the Clinical Theology Seminars. He has done years of work in primal therapy and has brought the healing balm of Jesus' understanding to many pained people.

His work with abreaction gives valuable insight into the depressed, hysterical, and schizoid personalities and homosexuality. He suggests that pre-natal and early post-natal experiences are far more formative than many people imagine. His insights have given us the courage to try and bring God's love to people whose history was far more traumatic than Gail's had been, and they have given us further understanding of some of the nagging problems which, though smaller, still resist change.

John Lehman and Russ Harris went to England to spend some time consulting with Frank Lake. One of the interesting things he pointed out to them was that there are some occasions when a person's improvement may be temporarily paradoxical—the person may feel like things are getting worse as he faces into the pain he's run from for years. This was observable in Gail's situation as she faced the prospect of accepting her mother's lack of attention. For a person who has had a much more damaging infant experience than hers, the challenge is much more traumatic, and he may wrestle with whether he is going to face into the pain. In those times of despair it is very tempting for the helpers to try and do something, anything to make the person feel better. One of the greatest temptations at that moment is to usher the person back into some kind of a delusion that everything is okay—he doesn't need to drink the cup of suffering. Put the lid back on and find some way of coping without healing. However, we must rely totally upon the Lord for our direction because an equally great temptation is the feeling of urgency to perform some kind of therapy. God's manner for healing the person may be less clinical; it may come unexplainably through the loving life around the person without any dramatic "cup of suffering." Only the Lord can show us which way to go.

There are other ways that we can hinder God's work by our fear of the depths. Several years ago some families came to the Fellowship which had been involved in a tangle of confusion, deep need, anger, and even adultery that threatened to destroy each family and individual involved. There was a great temptation to bring a premature closure to that situation by settling for superficial confessions and immediate forgiveness. But the people would have never been able to face each other in trust. The marriages might have teetered on for a while, but then they would have undoubtedly collapsed in ruin. Everyone would have been haunted by guilt for the rest of his life.

Instead, the counselors kept working on the understanding of everyone's responsibility, encouraging confessions and forgiveness when they were genuine, but never pronouncing the case closed until four and a half years later when a truly great celebration of trust and thankfulness took place. That's a long time. But the brothers and sisters would have been cheated by anything less. Actually, a good deal of distance from the situation had to happen before the people could even experience the depth of fear and pain that had been caused by the sin.

The couple most severely affected spent a portion of that time in separate communities in spite of the fact that they had four children. Then, as healing and trust increased, they both lived at Reba in a household under the careful oversight of the elders. But for some time they weren't ready to sleep together until healing, forgiveness, growing trust, and even a time of courtship had taken place. Their full reunification was a gracious and joyous gift from the Lord.

There are more d e p t h s to plumb. We have not learned how to banish very many problems with a simple rebuke. Maybe someday the Lord will teach us that. It is tempting to be too shallow and claim to have a deliverance ministry when it can't stand scrutiny. And it is tempting to avoid depth for fear that our own weaknesses will be revealed, but no true ministry is threatened by a confession of inadequacy or need on the part of the leaders. Not everyone has severe problems, but most of us have more needs than we've come to admit. A close life together will raise people's hopes that they are safe to experience their real selves.

We were painfully reminded of this not long ago. A young man came to us after the break up of his second marriage. He had been in and out of institutions, and we knew he had severe problems. He sought the Lord with as much hope as he had, and the Lord ministered to him in a real way. He lived in one of our households, and we all grew to love him deeply. He seemed to be making progress, and we believed we were doing everything we could do. But then one day his despair overwhelmed him. He slipped away, went up town, and jumped out of a fifth-story window to his death.

The first point of sobriety and integrity is to admit when one needs help. Develop resources! Plug into a network of communities where help is available. Get acquainted with the local mental health professionals, and use their services whenever possible. There are more Christians in the field than most people realize, and often non-Christian professionals will gladly cooperate if a church is conducting a sensible ministry. Many are quite aware of the need in our society for stable communities and are glad to see them in operation.

Also, be careful not to be overcome by fads—spiritual or secular. Seek balance. Each new insight that is useful and from the Lord should be added to a group's options for ministry. Be eclectic. No single approach will solve all problems, and all people do not have the same problem.

Finally, this chapter has concentrated on experience and depth because the Lord does not want us to be ignorant. But there is no substitute for His daily power and guidance. To paraphrase John, "The Lord was in the beginning; all things are known through him, and without him was not anything known that is known. In him is life, and the life is the light of men. The light shines in darkness, and the darkness does not overcome it."

14

Be Transformed

Within the context of the Christian community, there is the opportunity to experience many personal changes. Much of a person's spiritual growth is the result of good teaching—learning God's way. Some of it comes through being properly related to a body or local church —being in submission, developing gifts, etc. And some comes by sound pastoral care from brothers and sisters who are so deeply committed that a person can afford to expose his needs.

But there are a number of other benefits and opportunities for growth that aren't the result of vision, sound teaching, church order, counseling or fellowship. They are simply the products of living in the context of a Christian sub-culture where choices are possible. Some of these benefits have a spiritual value, and some are more practical in nature. Some of them can and do happen for the Christian who lives independently of other believers, but they are often easier in a body. They range all the way from having a way to recycle clothing for more efficient use to how funerals are conducted. The list could be long. I'll just mention a few points that I've noticed.

Grief and Separation

The experience of grief is one of the things that our society is losing its capacity to cope with, and many people suffer from unresolved experiences of grief or separation. At Reba Place we have given a great deal of attention to reclaiming old Christian traditions that help us get a right perspective on death and experience loss in a complete and genuine way. Such practices as homemade coffins, home viewing of the body, a community burial ground at our sister community, Plow Creek Fellowship, and loving reviews of the deceased person's life with lots of talk about feelings and many unashamed tears, all help process grief in a healthy way.

It has been known for a long time that when one doesn't adequately process the painful experiences of life, they stay with him and affect his future freedom. In terms of death people are often tempted to deny its reality, or they may be haunted by unreasonable fears, or they may be unable to enter into deep relationships with other people because they may have made a subconscious decision to never allow themselves to get so emotionally involved as to again be vulnerable to the pain of separation. That's an understandable response because no one likes to get burned twice, but in the long run it is not healthy. God wants us to accept the pain, experience it fully, and move on in life.

We have found this principle to be true in many experiences of life that are less traumatic than deaths. Whenever people move, change jobs, change groups, or for any reason have to leave a significant relationship or experience, it is important to be able to emotionally say good-bye. If it is not done fully, people are afraid to return or are always hankering to return and never content with the present. Or they may fear a repeat in the future.

In a community where there can both be teaching on the separation process and a group response, many good traditions and rituals can be created. For instance, when somebody moves from one household to another, we take a lot of time to process that. Not only do we carefully pray about it, talk it through and try to hear the Lord, but after we've made the decision, we usually set aside a time for a separation meal. Notes of appreciation and love are shared with the departing person; good times and hard times are remembered and discussed. Often people will write a poem or song or make a card or banner. And all the while the person is only moving down the street, and the whole household will see him again and again in the future, but with proper processing he can really make the shift. In the new household he is likely to be received with as much care.

Parenting by Model

In a society where independence is highly idealized, children tend to be programmed to go through a fairly severe rebellion just to accomplish growing up. Even though most parents expect their children to be obedient, independence must be achieved if that is the primary difference between childhood and adulthood. It logically follows that as the child matures in body and mind, he must face the challenge of resisting his parents in order to become the very kind of person they've exemplified, praised and taught him to become. In order to prove his passage the young person is nearly obligated to demonstrate his independence by some graphic departure from the life and norms of his parents. Young people sometimes suffer because of their recklessness at this point, and parents mourn without considering that they set their family up for that pain by their own example.

Within the church community which operates as the body of Christ, this problem does not need to be repeated generation after generation. Parents can offer a different model for adulthood. By their word and by their life they can declare that it is honorable, fulfilling and a privilege to live as an adult in submission to Jesus Christ. And they can demonstrate that it is appropriate to work that out by living in submission to others, especially others in the church. Children who see their parents joyfully doing this can find it more reasonable when they are required to obey. At least they are not receiving a double message. I'm much more comfortable in being able to say to my son, "I want you to be obedient to me just like you see me being obedient," than if I were saying one thing but living another.

Parenting by Cooperation

A community helps parents by making it possible to coordinate the environment for the children. For instance, one day we realized that our son Julian was into a pattern of watching a TV program that we didn't especially like. It wasn't very bad as TV goes, but as a steady diet we didn't think it was having a good influence on him. In setting out some new guidelines, we discovered that one of his main motives for watching it was that "all the other guys" watched it regularly and centered much of their play around recalling the previous episode, discussing it and re-enacting it. He claimed that he would be totally left out if he couldn't watch the show.

I could remember enough of my childhood to realize that there can be a good deal of real pain associated with being the "left-out one." So we called the parents of his best friends to test the validity of his claim that "everybody's doing it," and then considered with them whether we should all agree to limit the frequency that the boys watched the show. Because we were a small society formed by God, we could make some choices about the social environment that our children lived in and how we would approach their training.

Of course a young person needs to develop the strength to stand alone for what is right in the face of peer pressure, but in a worldly culture where the manipulation and pressures are so strong, a child can be harmed if that kind of separation is his constant experience. A child should have the experience of generally being accepted by those around him.

We can coordinate all kinds of things affecting our children—how late kids play out on the street, whether children are expected to do chores, and whether they should do some work over vacations. We can coordinate our response to the school or the PTA or almost anything that is beneficial and helpful to parenting.

Several communities have further developed this option by establishing schools for their children. This, of course, has often been one of the creative approaches that other Christian parents have taken to help raise their children.

Ethical Support in Business

At one community, a group of businessmen have organized an accountability group among themselves to help them run their businesses in ways that glorify the Lord. Their entire operations are opened to each other. Policy questions are tested by the brotherhood. Together they have changed many of their practices. Employee relations, advertising, credit, customer service, warranty faithfulness and taxes are all monitored so that the businessman is not forced through the pressure of competition to do things he doesn't really want to do before the Lord. He has the support of some fellow Christians to make the right choices and not to overextend himself and get in a bind. Even the kind of business that a person enters is discussed. Essential services are encouraged over luxury businesses.

Affirmation

We all need affirmation, and if we don't get it, we start seeking it. But in the world our search can go awry. We may need basic affirmation as a person but are only able to get affirmation through performance. That sometimes results in one part of a person's life soaring while another part crashes because no one cared enough to tell the person that even though he is good at his job, he'd better pay attention to the family.

Within a community where we are known more totally, affirmation can come in a more balanced way. For instance, suppose someone has a great deal of difficulty developing trusting relationships with other people yet seems to be a very spiritual person, spending long hours in meditation and always coming up with insights that sound profound and "words from the Lord." Among dedicated Christians who value spirituality it is easy for this kind of person to receive a great deal of affirmation for something that may be

154

an unhealthy means of escape. In a community where
the person's needs are known more fully, he can receive encouragement and affirmation for the brief
times when he does venture out in relationships because
others know that that is his area of need. They know
he is exercising real courage to take what may seem
to others like meager risks, and so they can support
him in reaching out.

Old Friends and Family

Not all prior relationships are enhanced by moving
into community. In fact, the intensity of involvement
in community life frequently results in not being able
to see prior friends and relatives as frequently. That
is a real sacrifice for the community members, and
it is sometimes a source of tension and disappointment
to those who are not living in the community. In the
New Testament Jesus talks about the willingness to
leave all the old comfortable relationships for the sake
of the Kingdom. And His disciples said, "We have done
just that." Then Jesus promised that His followers
would receive all those things multiplied a hundredfold
in the Kingdom in this life as well as eternal life.

In my experience that promise has literally come
true, and it has even happened in this life as Jesus
said it would. But He included a small qualifier—"with
persecutions" (Mark 10:30). There are times when that
technically happens to Christians, but if the word is
interpreted more broadly to mean pain, then I think
it is almost always fulfilled for the person who forsakes
all to follow Jesus.

One instance for me is the pain my commitment
has caused other relatives. I remember the day that
my sister said to me that it felt to her like I no longer
needed her as a sister, and that Julian and Rachel no
longer needed her as an aunt. We were so thoroughly
surrounded by brothers and sisters, aunts and uncles
in the Lord that we lacked no good thing, and she felt
unessential. Well, I really felt her pain in that statement. Actually, Julian and Rachel talk of her frequent-

ly, and we all love to be with her whenever we can. But I can understand what she was saying, and I am saddened by that.

I've thought of the time when Jesus declared the distinction between His own natural family and the spiritual family that had developed among those who were following Him. Some commentators think that His mother and brothers had come to talk Him out of His messianic role that was obviously heading Him toward a dangerous confrontation. But whether or not His family was offering a temptation that He needed to resist or just wanting to see Him, I'm sure He could see how much it was going to hurt them when He said, "Here are my mother and my brothers!" (referring to those who sat around Him). "Whoever does the will of God is my brother, and sister, and mother" (Mark 3:34, 35). And I'm sure His family's pain caused Him great sadness as well.

However, along with certain aspects of pain that come with the sacrifice of giving up everything to follow Jesus, there are also many benefits to family relationships that come from the healing of the Lord's life. We have known many instances where significant healing from guilts and resentments in a person's life has made possible the reconcilation of broken relationships with family members which had existed for years.

My relationship to my own parents has never been broken, but our visits were filled with tension for years as I tried to pressure them into accepting my ideas. I had never learned how to live very peacefully with those who disagreed with me. Coming from a somewhat fundamentalist background, I viewed "truth" as very important and "untruth," on almost any subject, as so dangerous that I tended to cut off trust and finally relationship with those who espoused "untruths." That approach left me over-invested in being right (so that I would not be cut off), and I was over-invested in making sure that those I loved were right (so that I would not have to cut them off).

Without knowing these causes, disagreements with my significant others raised dreadful separation anxieties within me and drove me back into discussion after discussion in hope of convincing them of what I had to say or of being convinced by what they had to say—I thought either conclusion would end the disagreement and dissolve my nearly subconscious but powerful fear.

It took some close brothers and sisters and some long counseling sessions to see how that dynamic operated in my life. But the insight has been very useful. Christ's message of reconciliation begins at home. I have learned the importance of affirming and enjoying what binds us together, rather than attacking our differences. I'm more at ease with letting my parents be themselves, appreciating who they are and realizing that our love and support for one another doesn't depend on thinking or doing things the same way. I think that they'd agree that our visits in the last couple years have become increasingly pleasant and peaceful.

Care for the Elderly

There is another very joyous aspect of life in community that some families are realizing. And that is the ability to provide a meaningful place for retired parents to live. Whether it is in a busy household or in a personal apartment nearby, grandparents are great to have around. They don't belong shut away in retirement homes. They belong in the middle of the community where they can share their hard-earned experience, where they can enjoy their grandchildren and other young people, and where they can receive the help and care they need from people they know and love rather than from some less interested persons in an institution.

Some older people are tired by the pace of small children and need a place of their own to relax, but it doesn't need to be far away. Others enjoy working part time. One grandparent at Reba is a tinsmith and puts in a few hours each day with the Just Builders construction crew. His health has improved so much since he came that the doctor sees him only twice a year instead of every month as was previously scheduled.

Some older people come with an interest in exploring the church life of the community with the possibility of becoming members. Others are not necessarily interested in membership and are here because it is not so lonely. Even when someone needs nursing care, that's usually available within the community.

In a community that lives in a close geographic proximity the older folks can go out for a walk and not be accosted by a mass of strange and uncaring faces. Half of the people they meet on the street usually know them and offer a friendly greeting.

Jesus had a special concern for older people. One of His last tasks before His death was to transfer His responsibility for the care of His mother to His brother John. He wanted to see that her needs were met.

There are many other benefits that could be listed for living in a community where you can make some choices about forming your environment and you are not totally at the mercy of the pressures of a secular culture. Some of the benefits are more meaningful to some people than others, but they are all valuable.

The other evening I noticed in the newspaper a full page ad picturing a smart looking "macho" man making his philosophical commentary on life: "Smoking is one thing. Taste is everything." I suppose that the ad agency doesn't think that they are going to convince very many people that the taste of a cigarette constitutes the totality of worthwhile human experience, but they had enough disrespect for our minds to say it and know that they could sell a lot of cigarettes by saying it long enough and loud enough. Truth and perspective were irrelevant to their goal.

When a company can mess with people's minds in that way and be successful in selling more people on their product than they horrify, it is a sad commentary on how punchy we've become.

We can be so buffeted by our environment that we're unable to make discernments about what is real or how we should live. Our Lord offers us help if we'll make our environment His church under His authority. That is the purpose of the body. According to Paul, it is in the context of the body that the power and gifts of the Spirit become active. There we are protected from being "tossed to and fro and carried about with every wind, . . . by the cunning of men, by their craftiness and deceitful wiles" (Eph. 4:14).

15

Singleness, Courtship and Marriage, an Example of Radical Choice

One of the most graphic examples of the radical benefits of a Kingdom sub-culture as experienced in a community is in the area of singleness, courtship and marriage. The individual Christian may desire to depart from the trends of the secular society around him and follow a more biblical approach in this area of life, but one can't change his courtship patterns unless others will change too. You can stop courting, but you can't court in a new way by yourself! It is a social interaction (as are many of our other experiences) and requires a societal transformation. And praise God, that can happen within the Christian community.

There are very few decisions that affect our lives and the lives of other people as much as the decision to marry. Few mistakes are as tragic as an ill-conceived marriage. Therefore, because the national divorce and unhappy marriage rates are so high, there is reason to question our whole contemporary approach. Many communities have done this and have totally rewritten modern practices and attitudes according to more Kingdom oriented standards. And they sound like a trip to another culture—because they are.

In many communities singleness is respected and honored as a unique service to the body. As Paul points out, the married person is frequently preoccupied with domestic responsibilites from which the single person is free. In the Word of God community there is a thriving group who have felt called to commit themselves to a celibate life within the community. They are understood to be "single for the Lord." After an extended period of testing that vocation in life, the whole community honors the person's public commitment with as much seriousness as marriage is celebrated. Steve Clark and Bruce Yocum, two of the coordinators for the community, are themselves "single for the Lord," and by their example have given special encouragement to this calling. Many other communities are following the example of the Word of God in formally recognizing commitments to singleness that free the individual from having to keep considering the question of marriage. However, even where there is not specific recognition, singles are fully involved and appreciated in the life of the community. They can share in and enjoy family life through a household when that seems best, or they can enter unreservedly into special ministry.

For those who are considering marriage, there are also new ways of approaching that question. First of all, because singleness is our original state, the decision to marry should not be presumed but should wait for a leading from the Lord. In the world great expectations and pressures are placed on the young person to find a mate and get married. In the Kingdom we can approach the topic differently. There need not be any pressure.

Because marriage is not the presumed goal for all young people, dating is not encouraged as the expected form of social adjustment. If courtship is discerned as God's will for someone, it is done seriously, not as a game played at over and over again with various partners for entertainment or experience. Entertainment and social adjustment take place in a community like Reba Place Fellowship in very lively group settings free from pairing off and the accompanying rivalries. Activities have ranged from regular get-togethers to a summer of working in the vegetable garden and living in tents at Plow Creek Fellowship, a long canoe trip in the wilderness, or a week visiting another community on the beach in Florida. Meaningful friendships with a number of people of both sexes are expected for everyone. Courtship or marriage is never seen as an escape or substitute for the person who has not developed these basic social skills.

Before anyone is encouraged to consider marriage, he should be a basically mature adult, healed of any severe problems that could shipwreck a marriage. This doesn't mean that he needs to be perfect; he just needs to have the tools to deal with the inevitable problems. For folks who have lived by worldly standards this frequently means a fairly thorough review, forgiveness, and healing of any previous relationships that were not Christian in nature. Other areas of maturity that are important to test are part of the person's stability in relationship to the Lord: Does he have reoccurring spiritual crises that have no reasonable source? Does he vacillate in his commitment to the church? Can he accept correction graciously? Is the person frequently into confusion about his life direction, unable to find satisfaction in a job or a comfortable place in the community?

The process of discerning the Lord's will and testing a person's preparedness for marriage is shared with the community. At Reba Place these questions come at some point to the person's small group. However, most of the searching takes place with the person's pastor. Sometimes the search begins when the person expresses an interest in exploring a "special relationship" with someone specific. Other times a person may just indicate a desire to be married. Occasionally the elders have suggested the names of several appropriate candidates, and the person then takes the initiative.

All members of the community have made life commitments to the Lord that preclude potential partners who have not made a similar commitment. This is primarily out of fairness to the partner. For instance, if a young person has totally committed his life to living under the lordship of Jesus with the understanding that his decisions are no longer private affairs but subject to testing in the body, then he has given the Lord a claim on his life which supersedes the wishes of a mate. If the mate was not also acknowledging Christ's lord-

ship in the same way, marriage would be an unfair
arrangement. Paul's counsel: "Do not be mismated
with unbelievers" (2 Cor. 6:14) is very wise in this respect. There is no problem with inter-community marriages (or marriage with any Christian similarly committed), since the lordship of Jesus and the authority
of the church is agreed upon. The only question is, "In
which community will the couple live?" The answer
is a matter of hearing the Lord.

Counsel is not suspended during courtship. Both
participants in the relationship share regularly about
how it is going so that no important issues are overlooked
or left unresolved. Prior to courtship both partners
should have matured from self-centeredness to a God-
centered and church-centered life. Courtship is a time
of testing whether that can remain true in the middle
of an intense relationship where there is a lot of temptation to be possessive and jealous. Marriage should
never become a substitute for a vital relationship to the
Lord or even a substitute for close and meaningful relationships to other people. Everyone has a deep driving
need to belong, be accepted, be loved, and find one's
place in life in terms of relationship and meaning.
Many, if not most, marriages have these as goals for
the relationship itself. But a spouse cannot deliver on
all these demands. In the long run disappointment and
decay set in, and the marriage is threatened. The Lord
is our only true source for meeting those needs. When
a couple is getting these needs met by the Lord, they
have more to give to each other and they are better
equipped to give to others, especially children. They can
accept children into their unit without feeling that their
source of life is being pillaged, and later they can open
their home in ministry to others by creating a larger
household if the Lord calls them to that.

In a very similar way a marriage must avoid an
emotional symbiosis so that both parties are not overwhelmed if one has struggles. There must be a sufficient degree of autonomy so that one partner can come
to the aid of the other.

All these areas should be worked out before the wedding, and so there is a good deal of counseling to aid the couple in getting started on the right foot. At Reba Place we have spent enormous amounts of time patching up broken marriages which come to us from the world's setting. We are grateful for this ministry, but it is expensive for all concerned. Sometimes when a family comes to us in a completely broken condition, they've asked that we care for their children for a period of time while they try to rebuild their marriage from the beginning. Though that has sometimes been better than leaving the children in the middle of the confusion, it's hard on them to go through that separation. It's also hard on those who care for the children, and it is hard on the parents. In every way it is better to invest time in building sound marriages the first time. It takes longer than the world's methods, but the rewards are great.

In the world the sexual side of a relationship often gets far ahead of the other aspects and commitments and even becomes the sole objective in many relationships. Playing with sex is inconsistent with Jesus' teaching that full physical intimacy belongs within the bond of the marriage covenant. Therefore, physical expressions of affection other than the hugs and other gestures normally common between all folks in the community are reserved for the latter stages of engagement leading to full union only after marriage. A little restraint pays off in much more objectivity during the time of testing and hearing the Lord about whether this is the right relationship or in discovering what things still need to be worked out before marriage.

Openness and honesty is a maxim for all relationships in the community, but it is particularly important during courtship, both between the couple and in the relationship to the rest of the community. In the world game-playing is often at its height between potential partners. It goes far beyond putting one's best foot forward. Sometimes there is a virtual masquerade, a pretense of being what one isn't or crass manipulation to "catch" a mate. In the Kingdom this kind of behavior, from flirting on up, is discouraged.

Openness and honesty must be the couple's response to the rest of the community as well. They are part of the body, and if they are united in marriage, the whole community will be affected. Courtship is actually a joyful experience that everyone contributes to and supports. The alienation and disapproval that courting couples experience in the world is often self-induced. One couple which was courting in our household mentioned that they were not feeling very supported. After a little exploration we were able to counsel them that people wanted to feel as welcome in their presence when they were together as before they began courting. If someone walked in the room and the couple's conversation stopped and hung like a dark cloud without the couple acknowledging and expressing joy at seeing the person, it was reasonable to expect that people would have reservations about the relationship. There would be a tendency to feel that their relationship was causing them to withdraw and close themselves off from their brothers and sisters. Nobody could feel good about that. The couple took the counsel to heart and began reaching out to others especially when they were together. Everyone's attitude about the relationship quickly changed. Others were being brought in on the relationship; they could support it; they could give feedback on how it was going. The couple was delighted.

And when the marriage took place, it was, as are all marriages at Reba Place, one of the biggest events you can imagine. The theme was "The Marriage of the Lamb," the model of Christ and His church. How we celebrated! Preparations began weeks before the wedding with nearly everyone participating. Each household contributed a service: one prepared the wedding food, one planned the rehearsal meal, one organized setting things up, one did clean up, another coordinated the guest hospitality, and on and on until everyone was participating. Guests came from other communities. Special music and dances were prepared. A song and dance was written especially for the couple. It is theirs and will remind the community of their wedding whenever it is sung in the future.

This revolutionary approach to courtship and marriage may seem a bit tedious, but it's been worth it by the testimony of those who have experienced it. We've sometimes joked that any couple which can run the gauntlet of the community's care during courtship can survive anything. But it's not that bad. They do get the experience of going through some difficult testings, but mostly it's very supportive and freeing. Singles can relate without the fear that every interaction is potentially an opportunity to attract a marriage partner or a failure to do so. And if they are not interested in marriage, they can have good friendships without always being misunderstood. And those who are interested in marriage don't have to fear that they are all alone, about to make some fatal mistake that will cause them years of pain and anguish.

However, the point of this example about marriage is that it requires a Kingdom sub-culture. These are social interactions and require the participation of several people in an agreed-upon Christian life-style in order for them to work. Many Christian young people, parents and pastors have desired some or all of these ideals, but they are nearly impossible to pull off alone, especially when we are constantly bombarded with propaganda that promotes non-Christian patterns for courtship and marriage.

If we are to be a people of God, we will have to allow Him to form us into a society.

16

Now, God's People

Once, many of us were no people. Now we are being formed into God's people. That's no credit to us. We are no better than anyone else. Many of us, in fact, were broken and needy when the Lord found us and began drawing us to himself and to each other.

But whether we are talking about the personal implications of coming together into church communities and the ways that God can use that setting to change us, or whether we are talking about the internal organization of our communities and the way God governs us, or whether we are trying to catch a glimpse of what He is doing in the world by bringing His church into unity, they all reflect His wonderful deeds in bringing us out of darkness into light. To give ourselves to that, to offer ourselves completely at His disposal is the only purpose for which life is worth living.

If our Lord is not bringing about His Kingdom in our hearts and lives, then we, among all people, are most pitiable. For we are in the process of giving up the most fetching attractions of this world's system— the promises to have all one can get and be one's own master.

But in fact, Christ *is* building His church, and the gates of hell and the strongholds of this world's system will not be able to stand against it. We are putting everything on the line for that.

Appendix A

A Selected List of Christian Communities

I was amazed as I compiled this list to see how many communities the Lord has been building. Not only is this list more than five times as long as the one in *Living Together*, but the average size of the communities I have selected is over 125 people, though smaller ventures are still proliferating. I have missed many communities (particularly those in Asia, Africa and South America), and have left others unlisted at their own request because they have been growing so rapidly that they cannot now absorb an increase in the rate of growth that further exposure might bring them.

My criteria for listing a community was not whether it was charismatic, had extended family households, a common purse or lived in a close geographic proximity; though those characteristics in one form or another are represented in most of these communities. What I looked for was whether the believers share a common life. Have they turned away from an individualistic existence to surrender all that they are and all that they have to Jesus via a local, self-conscious expression of His body?

By listing each of these communities I am not automatically endorsing all points of doctrine and practice in each one, but I have tried to eliminate cults. In most cases I have had some personal contact with each community or network and have also tested their basic Christian orthodoxy with some trustworthy person outside the group.

In this regard I am particularly indebted to Willy

Hubinont, who, because of his involvement in the late Centre Communautaire International, founded by Max Delespesse in Brussels, was able to provide me with information about many communities in Europe with which I was not otherwise familiar.

ALASKA

Gospel Outreach
3233 Tarrwater, Anchorage, Alaska 99504. *Phone:* (907) 272-7794
Contact person: Lambert Hazelaar
A fuller description of the Gospel Outreach Ministries can be found under the listing for Eureka, California. This branch in Anchorage began in 1973 and has about 120 people involved. There are two households, and the membership is primarily supported by a bakery and a professional cleaning and maintenance service.
Network: Gospel Outreach Ministries.

Maranatha North Church
P. O. Box 1108, Eagle River, Alaska 99577. *Phone:* (907) 688-2972
Contact person: Harold Dunaway
Network: This community is a member of the New Covenant Apostolic Order which is described under the listing for the Body of Christ Church, Indianapolis, Indiana.

ARIZONA

Canaan in the Desert
9849 North 40th Street, Phoenix, Arizona 85028. *Phone:* (602) 996-4040
Canaan in the Desert is a branch of the Evangelical Sisterhood of Mary, a fuller description of which can be found under the listing for their community in Germany.
Network: Evangelical Sisterhood of Mary.

People of Joy
7016 East Vista, Scottsdale, Arizona 85253. *Phone:* (602) 994-3557
Contact person: Jim Jones
Beginning initially, mostly from a Catholic charismatic prayer group, this community now includes people from many other denominations and has grown to a large size.

CALIFORNIA

Agape Fellowship
332 South Virgil Avenue, Los Angeles, California 90020. *Phone:* (213) 387-7881

Contact person: Tohru Dave Matsuo

Thirty-six covenanted members make up the core of this body of believers which began in 1971. They share a common purse and live in one apartment building. Their ministry is mostly to Asian Americans through various social services in their neighborhood and the publication of a magazine, The *Asian-American Journey.*

Network: They are informally related to the Berkeley Christian Coalition which publishes *Radix* from Berkeley, California.

City of the Angels

P.O. Box 45163, Los Angeles, California 90045. *Phone:* (213) 645-2271
Contact person: Charley Goraiebe

This community, initially beginning from charismatic prayer groups, now involves people from several denominational backgrounds in a full covenant life together.

The First Baptist Church of Chula Vista

494 "E" Street, Chula Vista, California 92010. *Phone:* (714) 422-0121
Contact person: Ken Pagard

This is a church renewed as a charismatic community with a number of households at the center of a larger congregation. The witness of their life together has given this community an important leadership role within their denomination and to various other smaller communities on the West Coast.

Gospel Outreach (Lighthouse Ranch Ministry)

1312 Beach Street, Eureka, California 95501. *Phone:* (707) 445-1546
Contact person: Larry Jamison

This community began in 1971 when about 30 young believers came together to transform an old Coast Guard lighthouse station into a Christian community as a base for fellowship and outreach. Under the guidance of Jim Durkin, they have grown until they now have communities in more than a dozen cities. This particular community has eight households and a total of more than 320 people involved in the fellowship. They support themselves through reforestation projects, professional cleaning services, the sale of pottery, the publication of an advertising paper and gardening.

Network: The unity among the Gospel Outreach communities in various cities is kept vital by a periodic gathering of all the presiding elders to share and give support and direction to the ministry. Also Jim Durkin and others offer oversight by visiting the different communities from time to time.

Gospel Outreach

1337 Murietta Drive, Apt. 3, Pomona, California 91768. *Phone:* (714) 629-7598
Contact person: Carmelo Bazzano

A fuller description of the Gospel Outreach Ministries can be found under the listing for Eureka, California. This branch in Pamona began in 1974 and has about 230 people involved. There are eleven households, and the membership is primarily supported by a leather and vinyl repair business, gardening, professional painting and cleaning services.

Network: Gospel Outreach Ministries.

Gospel Outreach

5402 Balboa Arms, Apt. 445, San Diego, California 92117. *Phone:* (714) 278-8823

Contact person: Ross Grove

A fuller description of the Gospel Outreach Ministries can be found under the listing for Eureka, California. This branch in San Diego began in 1975 and has about 130 people involved. There are two households, and the membership is primarily supported by a leather and vinyl repair business.

Network: Gospel Outreach Ministries.

Grace Catholic Church

6782a Pasado Road, Goleta, California 93017. *Phone:* (805) 968-4134

Contact person: Dean Brunner

Network: This community is a member of the New Covenant Apostolic Order which is described under the listing for the Body of Christ Church, Indianapolis, Indiana.

I'SOT Inc. (In Search Of Truth)

P. O. Box 125, Canby, California 96015. *Phone:* (916) 225-3841 or 3101

Contact person: E. Marie Tolbert

This community of approximately 150 people was established in 1960 in central California and later moved to Canby, a very small town in the northeast corner of the state where they purchased the remaining buildings and property of a burned-out lumber company. Their purpose is to promote the living and teachings of Jesus Christ, to provide a family environment where any who come to them may gain physically, mentally and spiritually what they may lack. They also desire to teach disciplined behavior, responsible thinking and help each person become emotionally stable. They have a unique and quite successful ministry in delinquency prevention, receiving both juvenile and adult placements from the courts and parents.

Mount Angelus Drive Fellowship

6276 Mt. Angelus Dr., Los Angeles, California 90042. *Phone:* (213) 255-9018

Contact person: Larry or Susan Jones

This very small group of people came together two years ago. They live in submission to a nearby church, the Highland Park Full Gospel Assembly.

Redeemer King Church
1709 Green Valley Road, Danville, California 94526. *Phone:* (415)
837-4564
Contact person: Bob Guio
Network: This community is a member of the New Covenant Apostolic Order which is described under the listing for the Body of Christ
Church, Indianapolis, Indiana.

COLORADO

Beyond Jordan
205 Logan, Denver, Colorado 80203. *Phone:* (303) 722-2372
Contact person: Billy Grissom
   The Beyond Jordan community of about 60 people has just completed a move from the St. Matthew's Parish in Houston, Texas,
to a somewhat depressed neighborhood in Denver. There they have
been welcomed by the Bishop to center their lives in St. Peter's
Church that has been declining and is in need of renewal. The Lord
has blessed them with four large houses side-by-side to be used as
households and several apartments and nuclear family units, all within easy walking distance of the church.
Network: This fellowship is a member of the Community of Communities, the *usually* parish-centered, fellowship-based circle of communities described in the first chapter of this book.

Community of Celebration
Box FF, Woodland Park, Colorado 80863. *Phone:* (303) 687-9237
Contact person: Grover Newman
   This community of almost 60 people provides the base for the
Fisherfolk traveling ministry team in the United States. The community was established in the fall of 1975 and realizes its financial
support through reforestry projects, conferences, contributions to the
Fisherfolk team, and the mail-order sales of teaching tapes, books,
sheet music, songbooks, records and handcrafted Celebration Jewel-
ry.
Network: This fellowship is a member of the Community of Communities, the *usually* parish-centered, fellowship-based circle of communities described in the first chapter of this book.

CONNECTICUT

Deer Spring (The Bruderhof)
Norfolk, Connecticut 06058. *Phone:* (203) 542-5545
   A description for the Bruderhof Communities may be found under
the entry for the Woodcrest Community in New York.
Network: The Bruderhof Communities, also known as the Hutterian
Society of Brothers, are part of the Hutterian Church.

GEORGIA

Alleluia Community

2321 Norton Court, Augusta, Georgia 30906. *Phone:* (404) 798-1882 or 790-5711

Contact person: Father Lou Lindsay

This large community began in about 1971 and involves people from several denominational backgrounds. They share a common purse among many of the people.

ILLINOIS

Austin Community Fellowship

5904 West Race Avenue, Chicago, Illinois 60644. *Phone:* (312) 287-2181

Contact person: Steve Adelsman

This community of nearly 30 people began in 1973 and currently has two households and other living units in the same neighborhood on the West Side of Chicago. As a group they currently attend Circle Church, an Evangelical Free Church in Chicago. Several members are involved in full-time neighborhood outreach sponsored by the church—medical clinic, legal aid clinic, etc.

Network: Austin Community Fellowship is exploring a relationship to the Shalom Covenant communities with Reba Place Fellowship and others fully described in the first chapter of this book.

Gospel Outreach

11 W. Delaware, Chicago, Illinois 60660. *Phone:* (312) 943-1254

Contact person: Charles Chambers

A fuller description of the Gospel Outreach Ministries can be found under the listing for Eureka, California. This branch in Chicago began in 1975 and has about 75 people involved. There are three households, and the membership is primarily supported by a leather and vinyl repair business, a leather shop and professional cleaning services.

Network: Gospel Outreach Ministries.

Jesus People U.S.A.

4431 N. Paulina, Chicago, Illinois 60640. *Phone:* (312) 728-4049

Contact person: Glenn Kaiser

This fellowship of nearly 200 people first began in the spring of 1972 in Milwaukee, Wisconsin. Later they migrated to Chicago, where, after a difficult start, they have flourished. The Lord has made available to them two apartment buildings, two houses, a church and recently a farm. Evangelism and discipleship training are the two main thrusts of their ministry as they have heard the Lord call them to live as a close-knit spiritual family, characterized by love.

Plow Creek Fellowship

Rt. 2, Box 2A, Tiskilwa, Illinois 61368. *Phone:* (815) 646-4505

Contact person: Conrad Wetzel

Plow Creek is a rural church community of about 65 people which began in 1971 when several families from Reba Place Fellowship were sent to begin a community on a newly purchased farm in central Illinois. The community is supported by a bakery, construction crew, gardening and several people who work at various jobs outside the community.

Network: Plow Creek is a part of the Shalom Covenant communities with Reba Place and others fully described in the first chapter of this book.

Reba Place Fellowship

727 Reba Place, Evanston, Illinois 60202. *Phone:* (312) 328-0772
Contact person: Peggy Belser, guest coordinator

This church community of about 300 people began in 1957. The 15 households and numerous nuclear family apartments are all located within walking distance. About half of the adults work in various jobs outside the community and the other half work within the community maintaining the life of the households, families, or ministries of counseling, neighborhood crafts for the youth, a day care center, low-cost housing, and others work on the construction crew or in oversight of the church life and outreach.

Network: Reba Place is part of the Shalom Covenant communities fully described in the first chapter of this book.

Salem Acres

Rt. 1. Rock City, Illinois 61070. *Phone:* (815) 449-2693
Contact person: Richard Rugg

Salem Acres is described by its members as a spiritual community or kibbutz located on an 80-acre farm in northern Illinois. They pattern themselves after the original assembly described in Acts 2:42-45. The community was established in 1970 and has been nurtured by the teachings of Lester Anderson into a "fundamental, Messianic and charismatic" life together. There are now about 120 people in the community.

Network: Salem Acres is related to communities in Rhinelander and Cameron, Wisconsin, and in England.

West Chicago

P. O. Box 396, West Chicago, Illinois 60185. *Phone:* (312) 393-1935
Contact person: Joe Friberg

A fuller description of the Daystar Ministries can be found under the listing for their center in Minneapolis, Minnesota. This branch in West Chicago is made up of about 60 people living in several households.

Network: Daystar Ministries.

174

INDIANA

Body of Christ Church

1334 South Reisner Street, Indianapolis, Indiana 46221. *Phone:* (317) 637-9473

Contact person: Ken Jensen

This community can best be described by the network of which it is a part.

Network: The New Covenant Apostlic Order is a newly emerging collection of as many as 100 small, previously independent, Christian bodies around the country. (This appendix lists only a representative few.) Through some early direction by Jack Sparks, Peter Gillquist and others the group felt deeply led to covenant themselves together under the reign of the Lord Jesus Christ. They do not see themselves in denominational terms but are striving for catholicity in their relationship to other existing churches and communions of churches. The Lord has turned them away from an independent spirit towards an interdependence and unity in the body of Christ where people are truly involved in all aspects of each other's lives. They desire to reflect the Kingdom of God as a light shining in the darkness by encouraging each church to be a living demonstration of the blessing and order of God's reign in contrast to the confusion and anarchy of Satan in a rebel world.

Daystar Campus Ministries

506 South High Street, P. O. Box 765, Bloomington, Indiana 47401. *Phone:* (812) 339-2600

Contact person: Dick Asp

A fuller description of the Daystar Ministries can be found under the listing for their center in Minneapolis, Minnesota. This branch in Bloomington is basically only one household and was established as housing for some of their students going to the university and as a base for a campus ministry to other students.

Network: Daystar Ministries.

Fellowship of Hope

414 W. Wolf, Elkhart, Indiana 46514. *Phone:* (219) 294-1416

Contact person: Keith Harder

This community of about 90 people began in 1970 when a small group of persons from a nearby Mennonite seminary were struggling to find meaning in their church experience. A common life together gradually led them to a corporate responsibility as a church. Most members work at jobs outside the community, many in the social services. Others run a nursery school, give oversight to the life and ministry of the community and do construction work, mechanics and gardening.

Network: Fellowship of Hope is a part of the Shalom Covenant communities with Reba Place Fellowship and others fully described in the first chapter of this book.

175

Martinsville Ministry Center
539 East Washington, P. O. Box 1514, Martinsville, Indiana 46151.
Phone: (317) 342-5591
Contact person: Jon Lyle
   A fuller description of the Daystar Ministries can be found under
the listing for their center in Minneapolis, Minnesota. This branch
in Martinsville is made up of about 120 people. As part of their outreach they offer three 3-month Christian maturity seminars each year
as well as weekend retreats.
Network: Daystar Ministries.

People of Praise
237 North Michigan Street, South Bend, Indiana 46601. *Phone:* (219)
287-5961
Contact person: John Burke
   In 1971 a number of people who had been touched by the charismatic renewal met regularly for six weeks to seek the Lord about
His will for their lives. Convinced that the Lord wanted them to make
an unreserved commitment to Him and to each other, 29 people became the first covenant members of the People of Praise. Since then
the community has grown to include hundreds of other people in
many living situations around the city in residential and nonresidential households according to what suits each individual's needs and
gifts best.
Network: People of Praise is a member of the covenant of ecumenical
communities.

KANSAS

Marion Mennonite Brethren Church
307 South Washington, Hillsboro, Kansas 67063. *Phone:* (316) 947-
5452
Contact person: John Ratzlaff
   There are about 45 people living in community within this congregation initially established as a church in 1898. The church had periods of growth and decline and almost died until 1969 when renewal
first began with acceptance of the baptism of the Holy Spirit. In
1975 several of the members were led to share their lives in community. Since then the life and ministry of the congregation has been
substantially strengthened and expanded.
Network: This church community is exploring a relationship with
the Shalom Covenant communities of which Reba Place Fellowship
is a part. The circle is fully described in the first chapter of this
book.

New Creation Fellowship
417 W. 11th Street, Newton, Kansas 67114. *Phone:* (316) 283-1363
Contact person: Jake Pauls

This community of about 70 people is made up of three extended-family households and various nuclear family living units all within the same neighborhood. The community is supported by outside jobs primarily, freeing several people to work within the community. These Christians have joined together in order to commit their lives totally to Jesus Christ. God has blessed them by healing marriages, freeing people to use their gifts and bringing others to Himself.

Network: New Creation Fellowship is a part of the Shalom Covenant communities with Reba Place Fellowship and others fully described in the first chapter of this book.

LOUISIANA

Jesus the King Community

4920 Kent Avenue, Metairie, Louisiana 70002. *Phone:* (504) 455-1361
Contact person: Al Mansfield

This is a large community involving people from many denominations.

MARYLAND

Lamb of God

11501 Jennifier Road, Timonium, Maryland 21093. *Phone:* (301) 252-4947 or 252-4988
Contact person: Guest master

This large community in a suburb north of Baltimore is made up of Protestants, Catholics and Jewish Christians experiencing the unity that Christ wants for Christians. The members of the community, which began in a formal way in 1973, enjoy a variety of living situations according to the needs of each individual. Some live in extended family households; others live as nuclear families or singles and meet together regularly for prayer, mutual support and accountability.

Network: Lamb of God is a member of the covenant of ecumenical communities.

MASSACHUSETTS

The Community of Jesus

Rock Harbor, Orleans, Massachusetts 02653. *Phone:* (617) 255-1094
Contact person: Hal M. Helms

This community of about 180 people was founded in 1970 by Cay Andersen and Judy Sorensen. There are 15 households comprising the residential community plus a sisters' dormitory and a retreat house. They have a sisterhood of 25 sisters and a brotherhood of 10 brothers (in the usual monastic sense). They engage in an active retreat ministry for laity and clergy plus counselling and teaching programs. There is a "live-in" arrangement for people who want to spend as much as two weeks to a year receiving intensive help in their personal lives. They hold a public teaching meeting on Monday evenings and daily communion led by an Episcopal priest.

MICHIGAN

Beth-El Village

17425 Long Lake Highway, Alpena, Michigan 49707. *Phone:* (517) 595-6545
Contact person: Wally Englund
A fuller description of the Daystar Ministries can be found under the listing for their center in Minneapolis, Minnesota. This branch in Alpena is made up of about 50 people and has as its primary outreach the sponsoring of retreats.
Network: Daystar Ministries.

Christ's Community

242 Carlton Southeast, Grand Rapids, Michigan 49506. *Phone:* (616) 459-1952
Contact person: Gene Beerens
This community began in Terre Haute, Indiana, in 1970 and moved while their size was very small to Grand Rapids in 1973 where rapid growth has brought their number to around 250 people in a Christian Reformed Church parish. There are eight households and about half of the people share a common purse supported partially by an automobile service station, woodworking and furniture making shop, a maintenance and remodeling crew. Their community has a strong conviction about the importance of standing for social and economic justice by sharing their community with the poor and oppressed and challenging the culture and life-style of many affluent Christians in North America.
Network: This fellowship is a member of the Community of Communities, the *usually* parish-centered, fellowship-based circle of communities described in the first chapter of this book. They also maintain strong, though informal, ties with Reba Place Fellowship and other communities.

Church of the Messiah

231 East Grand Boulevard, Detroit, Michigan 48207. *Phone:* (313) 567-1158
Contact person: Ron Spann
This is a family life-style fellowship within an Episcopal parish. There are about 200 people involved. The renewal of the parish and

the beginning of the community was greatly aided by the ministry of the Church of the Redeemer in Houston, Texas. The fellowship includes several extended family households, an elementary school, day-care center, ministry to retarded and emotionally disturbed people in nearby foster care facilities, a strong neighborhood outreach and a renewal ministry to other churches and communities.

Network: This fellowship is a member of the Community of Communities, the *usually* parish-centered, fellowship-based circle of communities described in the first chapter of this book. They also maintain strong, though informal, ties with Reba Place Fellowship and other communities.

Menominee River Fellowship

2116 11th Avenue, Menominee, Michigan 49858. *Phone:* (906) 864-2387
Contact person: Paul Versluis

This lively group of about 60 people began in 1975 when a couple families, formerly associated with the People's Christian Coalition, moved to Menominee with the desire to begin a Christian community. The Lord has blessed them by expanding their church group and giving them a food co-op, coffeehouse youth ministry, Bible studies, and bookstore. They welcome new members and seekers; though life in their econmically depressed area is not easy.

Network: They are associated with the Community of Communities, the *usually* parish-centered, fellowship-based circle of communities described in the first chapter of this book.

St. Gregory's Abbey

Rt. 3, Box 330, Three Rivers, Michigan 49093. *Phone:* (616) 244-5893
Contact person: Anthony Damron, Prior

This Benedictine order was established in 1939, and the 20 men who make up the farming and prayer community lead a disciplined monastic life. They are the only Benedictine monks in North America who are not in the Roman Catholic Church. They are members of the Episcopal Church but maintain close ties with several religious communities in both communions. The abbey serves as a retreat center for many individuals and groups.

The Word of God

P. O. Box 7087, Ann Arbor, Michigan 48107. *Phone:* (313) 668-4694
Contact person: Jene Firn

The Word of God had its beginnings in 1967 when 15 people gathered for a prayer meeting near the University of Michigan. In response to a prophecy from the Lord asking them to covenant themselves together, about 70 people made that full commitment in 1969. Since that time the community has grown to become probably the largest Christian community in the country with hundreds of people in the Ann Arbor area. To maintain their close sense of love and body life, the Lord has led them to develop many smaller groupings within their total number. These minister to people according to their needs through residential or nonresidential households to facilitate the member's opportunity to discover and do the Lord's will and realize His love and care on a daily basis.

Network: Word of God is a member of the covenant of ecumenical communities.

Work of Christ

P. O. Box 392, East Lansing, Michigan 48823. *Phone:* (517) 351-2700
Contact person: Jerry Munk

From their initial beginnings as a charismatic prayer group in about 1967, this group first developed into a covenanted community in the early 1970's. Since then it has grown into a very large and healthy community involving people from many denominational backgrounds.

Network: Work of Christ is a member of the covenant of ecumenical communities.

MINNESOTA

A Christian Family

Rt. 1, Box 109, Guthrie, Minnesota 56451. *Phone:* (218) 224-2173
Contact person: Steve Scott

This group of about 40 people moved from California and Utah to this Minnesota farm in October 1973—just in time to see how harsh a winter in the north can be when you are tight on food and have to arrange make-shift housing. Six of the men slept in a tent which they heated by burning old tires that first winter. Since then they have been helped by the Hutterites from Forest River, North Dakota, and have built a large three-story common building and other facilities. Their desire is to be a "city on a hill" living out the gospel of Jesus Christ.

Bethany Fellowship

6820 Auto Club Rd., Minneapolis, Minnesota 55438. *Phone:* (612) 944-2121
Contact person: Alec Brooks

This missionary-minded community grew out of a church congregation in 1945. Just 16 members received a missionary challenge to train, send and support 100 foreign missionaries. Now 490 people are involved in the Fellowship. The goal of 100 missionaries has been reached and almost doubled. It has happened because the believers were willing to sell all of their possessions, pool their resources and work full time in the training center, publishing division or industry which manufactures camping trailers, electrical appliances and other electronic equipment.

180

Daystar Ministry Center

4500 Minnetonka Boulevard, Minneapolis, Minnesota 55416. *Phone:*
(612) 920-1317
Contact person: Larry Ballard
  The Daystar Ministries began in 1964 in this community under
the direction of Jack Winter. The group has since branched out to
more than a dozen locations with different emphases: a family camp
and retreat center, discipleship training school, missionary retreat
center, conferences, cassette tape and videotape ministry, Christian
maturity seminars, and in each community a strong counseling ministry. They desire to facilitate the maturity of the body of Christ
among themselves and for those who come to them through teaching
(with a strong emphasis on the importance of dying to self); personal
ministry to individuals and families in the form of deliverance, counseling and inner healing; and through the love, care, and shepherding
which is integral to their common life. This particular community
in Minneapolis has about 45 people living in it and has its main emphasis on counseling. They share a common purse among the members.
Network: The Daystar Ministries is a close network coordinated
through meetings of the leadership at least three times each year.
People also freely move from center to center according to where
their gifts are most needed in the ministry. Several of their communities have schools, primarily set up for their children, grades
K-12.

Highland House

3881 Highland Avenue, N., Saint Paul, Minnesota 55110. *Phone:*
(612) 426-3911
Contact person: Kip Jentoft
  A fuller description of the Daystar Ministries can be found under
the listing for their center in Minneapolis, Minnesota. This branch
in Saint Paul is made up of about 25 people living in households.
Network: Daystar Ministries.

Zion Harbor

Federal Dam, Minnesota 56641. *Phone:* (218) 654-3602
Contact person: Jesse Good
  A fuller description of the Daystar Ministries can be found under
the listing for their center in Minneapolis, Minnesota. This branch
at Federal Dam is made up of about 100 people who operate a camp
and retreat center.
Network: Daystar Ministries.

Servants of the Light

4744 Grand Avenue South, Minneapolis, Minnesota 44509. *Phone:*
(612) 827-2811
Contact person: Dennis Rayl
  This is a very large community, divided into districts according
to where the people live so that there can be a close brotherhood.

The community began in 1971 when a number of people who had been meeting in a charismatic prayer group committed their lives to one another. "All that we have and all that we are doing, we give to God and to each other until the body sees differently," they said to one another. Since then the community's size as well as its ministry has grown dramatically.

Network: Servants of the Light is a member of the covenant of ecumenical communities.

MISSISSIPPI

New Covenant Catholic Church
1012-B Poplar, Jackson, Mississippi. *Phone:* (601) 355-1894
Contact person: Dale Autrey
Network: This community is a member of the New Covenant Apostolic Order which is described under the listing for the Body of Christ Church, Indianapolis, Indiana.

Voice of Calvary
1655 Saint Charles Street, Jackson, Mississippi 39209. *Phone:* (601) 353-1635
Contact persons: Phil Reed, Artis Fletcher or Dolphus Weary

The Voice of Calvary consists of two individual churches, one in Mendenhall and the other in Jackson. Voice of Calvary began in Mendenhall in 1960 in the poor black neighborhood where John and Vera Mae Perkins wanted to meet the physical as well as the spiritual needs of the people. The church now operates a medical clinic, gymnasium, library, cafeteria and new thrift store in Mendenhall. In 1975 another branch of the community was begun in Jackson where the ministry includes the renovation and low-cost sale or rental of previously deteriorating houses, a youth center and a ministry on Jackson State University campus.

Network: This fellowship is a member of the Community of Communities, the *usually* parish-centered, fellowship-based circle of communities described in the first chapter of this book.

MISSOURI

The Covenant Community at Broadway Baptist Church
4 East 69th Street, Kansas City, Missouri 64113. *Phone:* (816) 333-7815
Contact person: Dick Simmons

For several years Broadway Baptist Church in Kansas City has been divided into a number of koinonia groups to help facilitate fellowship and support. Recently some of the people in the church have been drawn into a deeper covenant and accountability to each other in the form of community life.

182

Network: This group is exploring a relationship with the Shalom Covenant communities connected with Reba Place Fellowship. That circle is fully described in the first chapter of this book.

NEW JERSEY

People of Hope
Xavier Center, Convent Station, New Jersey 07103. *Phone:* (201) 267-0617
Contact person: Robert Gallic or James J. Ferry
This is a large, mostly Catholic community of people who have covenanted their lives together to seek and do the Lord's will.

NEW YORK

Gospel Outreach
317 Park Avenue, Freeport, New York 11520. *Phone:* (516) 623-3050
Contact person: Tom Kennedy
A fuller description of the Gospel Outreach Ministries can be found under the listing for Eureka, California. This branch in Freeport began in 1974 and has about 140 people involved. There are three households, and the membership is primarily supported by a leather and vinyl repair business and outside jobs.
Network: Gospel Outreach Ministries.

Gospel Outreach
Rt. 5, West River Road, Oswego, New York 13126. *Phone:* (315) 343-6550
Contact person: Paul Wagner
A fuller description of the Gospel Outreach Ministries can be found under the listing for Eureka, California. This branch in Oswego began in 1975 and has about 100 people involved. There is one household, and the members primarily support themselves through the New Life Services Company.
Network: Gospel Outreach Ministries.

Household of Faith
2235 University Avenue, Bronx, New York 10453. *Phone:* (212) 733-0416
Contact person: Jack Roberts
The Household of Faith is a house church that began in 1971 and now involves about 50 people. Half of those are adult, covenanted members, several of whom live in two extended-family households. Some members of the community work in a residential drug addiction treatment program, Hope Christian Center.
Network: They are exploring relationships with other nearby fellowships.

Love Inn Ministries

Rt. 2, Freeville, New York 13068. *Phone:* (607) 347-4411

Contact person: Jim Harrington

This community of about 270 people began in 1970 with a dynamic coffee-house ministry under the direction of Scott Ross. They now enjoy a fairly full community life and ministry in many areas. The group is divided into eleven small groups that meet regularly to help discern the Lord's will for each individual. They have a school, kindergarten through eighth grade.

Woodcrest (The Bruderhof)

Rifton, New York 12471. *Phone:* (914) 658-6561

In 1920, a small group of Christians led by Eberhard and Emmy Arnold began community life in the little village of Sannerz in Germany. After years of crisis and growth, the group was chased from Germany by Hitler, first to settle in England, then to migrate to Paraguay, and finally to the United States where there are now three settlements. They have also established a settlement in England. From their small beginning in Germany they have grown to well over a thousand people from all manner of backgrounds who are committed to a life of love as followers of Christ. This commitment means giving up all property and self interest. No individual tries to achieve all he can for himself. The community supports itself financially by the production of Community Playthings, the wooden toys which are highly respected for their sturdiness and versatility in day-care centers and nursury schools throughout this country and Europe. They share much of their life and vision through books, pamphlets and records produced by the Plough Publishing House. Visitors who are open and seeking are welcome to share in their life and work. However, because of the number that they host, they request each guest to make arrangements in advance.

Network: The other Bruderhof settlements are: New Meadow Run in Pennsylvania, Deer Spring in Connecticut, and Darvell in England. (See individual listings for addresses.) The Bruderhof Communities are officially known as the Hutterian Society of Brothers, indicating the remarkable uniting they experienced with the Hutterian Church in 1974. (See the first chapter of this book for a description.)

NORTH DAKOTA

Daystar—Gardner

P. O. Box 2542, Fargo, North Dakota 58102. *Phone:* (701) 293-3500

Contact person: Luther Matsen

A fuller description of the Daystar Ministries can be found under the listing for their center in Minneapolis, Minnesota. This branch in Fargo is made up of about 120 people who live in a five-story hotel and operate it as a conference center.

Network: Daystar Ministries.

184

Forest River Colony

Fordville, North Dakota 58231. *Phone:* (701) 865-4166
Contact person: Joe W. Maendel, minister

Forest River is one of the many Hutterite communities in the United States and Canada. (There are about 25,000 Hutterites in North America.) Like all Hutterite communities, Forest River is primarily a farming colony, living out their rich, 400-year-old tradition in a quiet but industrious way.

Network: Though there are sub-groupings within the Hutterite Church, all of the more than 200 colonies are in basic unity with each other and now with the Society of Brothers.

OHIO

New Covenant Fellowship

Rt. 3, Box 213A, Athens, Ohio 45701. *Phone:* (614) 592-4605
Contact person: Cordell Bowman

This small community of 18 people is now located on a 120-acre farm in Ohio after moving from southeast Kentucky where they began in 1973. The main focus of the community is to seek first God's Kingdom, to follow Jesus in every area of life, with the understanding that this is best discerned and lived out as a gathered body. They have been challenged to seek a simpler life-style, reduce consumption, identify with the poor and not pay war taxes.

Network: They have an informal relationship with the Society of Brothers and Reba Place Fellowship.

New Jerusalem Community

745 Derby Avenue, Cincinnati, Ohio 45232. *Phone:* (513) 541-4748
Contact person: The guestmaster.

This is a Catholic community of about 400 people, 170 of whom live in the same neighborhood in a variety of living situations: families, extended families, households, and smaller groups of caring relationships. The people in about 12 extended family households live much like the early Christians in that they regularly pray, share and support each other. They provide a corporate and visible witness of the Body of Christ, and their simple life-style allows them to free about 25 people for full-time ministry. Father Richard Rohr, one of the pastors in the community, has been an important inspiration to their life together since they began in 1973. They are not a covenant community.

Servants of God's Love

814 Longford Drive, Steubenville, Ohio 43952. *Phone:* (614) 282-6640
Contact person: Tom Kneier

More than 100 people are involved in this community near the College of Steubenville. Many are faculty, staff and students at the college.

Son of God Community
2999 West 12th Street, Cleveland, Ohio 44113. *Phone:* (216) 687-1363
Contact person: Raymond Kress
This Roman Catholic community of about 180 people grew up in 1973 next to a parish in the near west inner city of Cleveland. Physically the area is surrounded by three steel mills and several freeways, but their life together has grown as they have committed themselves to lay down their lives, both spiritually and physically, in a way similar to the example of Jesus' submission to the Father. From that goal came their name, Son of God. They sponsor a Montessori School and work together to make area housing livable. They also have a food ministry to the people living around them consisting of free meals and a catering service for special events.
Network: They are exploring the possibility of formally relating to the Community of Communities, the *usually* parish-centered, fellowship-based circle of communities described in the first chapter of this book.

University Christian Fellowship Church
397 East 17th Avenue, Columbus, Ohio 43201. *Phone:* (614) 294-7256
Contact person: Mike Seiler
Network: This community is a member of the New Covenant Apostolic Order which is described under the listing for the Body of Christ Church, Indianapolis, Indiana.

OKLAHOMA

Daystar Ministries
25 East 22nd Street, Tulsa, Oklahoma 74114. *Phone:* (918) 585-2869
Contact person: Merland Severson
A fuller description of the Daystar Ministries can be found under the listing for their center in Minneapolis, Minnesota. This branch in Tulsa is made up of about 20 people. They have been recently established and have not yet defined what the Lord wants their outreach to be.
Network: Daystar Ministries.

OREGON

Gospel Outreach
611 N.W. "A" Street, Grants Pass, Oregon 97526. *Phone:* (503) 476-2167
Contact person: Wally Sharp
A fuller description of the Gospel Outreach Ministries can be found under the listing for Eureka, California. This branch in Grants Pass began in 1976 and has about 90 people involved. There are two house-

holds, and the membership is primarily supported by a leather and vinyl repair business.
Network: Gospel Outreach Ministries.

Gospel Outreach

602 Oak Street, Silverton, Oregon 97381. *Phone:* (503) 873-5795
Contact person: Ed Montgomery
 A fuller description of the Gospel Outreach Ministries can be found under the listing for Eureka, California. This branch in Silverton began in 1974 and has about 95 people involved. There are two households, and the membership is primarily supported through businesses in professional painting and cleaning services.
Network: Gospel Outreach Ministries.

Orchard Street Church

1598 Orchard Street, Eugene, Oregon 97403. *Phone:* (503) 344-3163
Contact person: Stuart Smith, pastor
 This church of more than 60 people began in 1970 and has several communal households as well as support groups within the larger congregation. There is a strong emphasis on discipleship and some ministry to the nearby University of Oregon campus.

Shekinah

Rt. 1, Box 67, Logsden, Oregon 97357. *Phone:* (503) 444-2228
Contact person: Allen J. Yoder
 Shekinah is a community-oriented discipleship school where the students and staff share a common life together under the oversight of the elders of the Logsden Mennonite Church, of which the community is a part. Though the community is very new, with just a few families and singles, it is patterned after Bethany Fellowship with the school, students and staff and those sent out in ministry being supported by a common industry of cabinet and furniture making and house construction.

PENNSYLVANIA

Gospel Outreach

8686 Bustleton, Philadelphia, Pennsylvania 19115. *Phone:* (215) 464-1924
Contact person: Chris Pritchard
 A fuller description of the Gospel Outreach Ministries can be found under the listing for Eureka, California. This branch in Philadelphia began in 1977 and has about 50 people involved. There is one household, and the membership is primarily supported through a leather and vinyl repair business.
Network: Gospel Outreach Ministries.

Jubilee Fellowship of Germantown

312 West Logan Street, Philadelphia, Pennsylvania 19144. *Phone:* (215) Vi3-9269

Contact person: Arbutus B. Sider

This community of about 45 people began in the summer of 1974. They now all live within easy walking distance of each other in a multiracial neighborhood where they feel called to affirm the gospel of jubilee by proclaiming "the year of the Lord's favor" (Luke 4:14-18) and "liberty throughout the land" (Lev. 25:10). Besides their church life together, they have tried to express the spirit of jubilee by involvement in their neighborhood by helping people buy and renovate abandoned, government-owned buildings. Their fellowship also participates in the publication of *The Other Side* magazine, the leading of discipleship workshops in other churches, Liberty to the Captives (designed to get laws passed that will stop our government from supporting repressive regimes), and Jubilee Crafts.

Network: This fellowship is considering membership in the Community of Communities, the *usually* parish-centered, fellowship-based circle of communities described in the first chapter of this book.

New Meadow Run (The Bruderhof)

Farmington, Pennsylvania 15437. *Phone:* (412) 329-5515

A description for the Bruderhof Communities may be found under the entry for the Woodcrest Community in New York.

Network: The Bruderhof Communities, also known as the Hutterian Society of Brothers, are part of the Hutterian Church.

TENNESSEE

Grace Church

4023-B Aberdeen Road, Nashville, Tennessee 37205. *Phone:* (615) 298-3844

Contact person: Jack Howe

Network: This community is a member of the New Covenant Apostolic Order which is described under the listing for the Body of Christ Church, Indianapolis, Indiana.

TEXAS

Church of the Redeemer

4411 Dallas St., Houston, Texas 77023. *Phone:* (713) 928-3221

Contact person: Roger Gumbinner

A church attended by 950 persons, about 190 of whom are living in 22 extended-family households. A dying church in 1965, Church of the Redeemer has experienced miraculous renewal through the power of the Holy Spirit, and today is a thriving and ministering body. The experience of this church has affected many other churches and communities.

Community of God's Delight
4530 San Gabriel, Dallas, Texas 75229. *Phone:* (214) 653-1826
Contact person: Bobbie Cavnar
   This large charismatic community had Episcopal roots; however, it is now ecumenical and experiencing the unity between Christians that Jesus prayed for in John 17.

Grace Community Church
7479 Walling Lane, Dallas, Texas 75231. *Phone:* (214) 341-5422
Contact person: Robin Madaway
Network: This community is a member of the New Covenant Apostolic Order which is described under the listing for the Body of Christ Church, Indianapolis, Indiana.

Harmony Hill
Box 136, Mercedes, Texas 78570. *Phone:* (512) 565-3217
Contact person: Don Edson
   A fuller description of the Daystar Ministries can be found under the listing for their center in Minneapolis, Minnesota. This branch in Mercedes is made up of about 45 people who staff it as a missionary retreat center.
Network: Daystar Ministries.

WASHINGTON

Gospel Outreach
1916 Orange, Olympia, Washington 98501. *Phone:* (206) 943-7563
Contact person: Don O'Connor
   A fuller description of the Gospel Outreach Ministries can be found under the listing for Eureka, California. This branch in Olympia began in 1975 and has about 35 people involved. There are three households, and the membership is primarily supported by a cleaning service business.
Network: Gospel Outreach Ministries.

Gospel Outreach
1733 15th Avenue, Seattle, Washington 98122. *Phone:* (206) 325-3203
Contact person: Paul Dixon
   A fuller description of the Gospel Outreach Ministries can be found under the listing for Eureka, California. This branch in Seattle began in 1975 and has about 85 people involved. There are four households, and the membership is primarily supported by a rug cleaning service, and other service industries.
Network: Gospel Outreach Ministries.

Seattle Church
Phone: (206) 783-8821
Contact person: Ken Berven
Network: This community is a member of the New Covenant Apostolic Order which is described under the listing for the Body of Christ Church, Indianapolis, Indiana.

WASHINGTON, D. C.

Sojourner's Fellowship
1343 Euclid Street, NW, Washington, D. C. 20009. *Phone:* (202) 232-2586
Contact person: Bob Sabath
This community of about 50 people was formerly known as the People's Christian Coalition, living in Deerfield, Illinois, and publishing the *Post-American* newspaper. Since moving to Washington, D.C., the community has been renamed Sojourner's Fellowship, and the publication is now known as *Sojourners* magazine. It is edited by Jim Wallis, 1029 Vermont Avenue, NW, Washington, D. C. 20005, one of the other community houses. The community has felt a strong burden to integrate the pastoral and prophetic aspects of their life. They live in a depressed neighborhood where they are called upon constantly to minister to the people and needs around them. There are also pastoral needs within their own community, and yet they have a strong call to speak prophetically to broader issues in our world. The magazine, speaking engagements around the country and educational campaigns on nuclear arms and energy, human rights and other issues are some of the ways they address this responsibility.
Network: This fellowship is a member of the Community of Communities, the *usually* parish-centered, fellowship-based circle of communities described in the first chapter of this book.

WISCONSIN

Eden Ministry Center
Box 110, Rt. 1, Weyerhauser, Wisconsin 54895. *Phone:* (715) 353-2280
Contact person: Bill Lemke
A fuller description of the Daystar Ministries can be found under the listing for their center in Minneapolis, Minnesota. This branch in Weyerhauser is the discipleship training school for the other communities. The training sessions last about a year. There are 10 staff members and about 30 students most of the time.
Network: Daystar Ministries.

AUSTRALIA

The Buttery

P. O. Box 36, Bangalow, New South Wales 2479, Australia. *Phone:* 066-8731

Contact person: John McKnight

This community began in about 1973 when the people involved were able to rent an old disused butter factory. They have a vision for further evangelism (particularly among counter-culture people), the care of each other as the body of Christ and concern for various social concerns. They are developing extended family households around their original building and hope to support a traveling team.

Emmanuel

National Communications Office, No. 8, Bateman Street, Geebung 4034 Brisbane, Queensland, Australia

Contact person: Brian Smith

This well-established community of several hundred people is covenanted together to express God's love. They are divided into smaller groups so as to keep the intimacy of the body of Christ, yet they can all work together in ministry. Recently they were joined by about 80 people who moved across the continent to join them and strengthen their witness.

Essendon Baptist Church

134 Buckley Street, Essendon, Victoria 3040, Australia. *Phone:* 337-5653

Contact person: Dick Littleton

This church has been interested in developing a closer life together, caring for one another as the body of Christ and seeking the Lord's will together.

Jacob's Ladder Christian Community

102 Gawler Place, Adelaide, South Australia 5000, Australia. *Phone:* 223-6684

Contact person: Doug Kuhl

This community, which was established in 1973, has about ten community houses situated in the inner suburb of Adelaide. There most of the members live and minister through a drop-in center, coffee house, library and worship center. Through the ministry of the gifts of the Holy Spirit, their work has touched a large number of people.

Jesus Centre-Adelaide

61 Sydenham Road, Norwood, 5067 South Australia, Australia. *Phone:* 425-904

Contact person: Malcolm Graetz

This small group of Christians have been together since 1972. They have been led into areas of community living, teaching and functioning as a church body.

Malabar Parish Community

St. Mark's Church, Franklin Street, Malabar, New South Wales 2036, Australia

Contact person: Steve Lawrence

This is a newly formed community at the core of a parish church. They are a closely committed group of people, living together, encouraging one another as well as sharing decision making and finances. Their vision is to encourage renewal within their whole church.

CANADA

Bread of Life Community

617 McKenzie Road, Abbotsford, British Columbia, V2S 4N2. *Phone:* (604) 859-5507

Contact person: Herb Klassen

This group of families, mostly from Mennonite backgrounds, experienced the charismatic renewal and began drawing closer in a fellowship life together. As they have joined their lives and many of their resources together in a rural setting, the Lord has led them into a substantial prison ministry.

Community Farm of the Brethren

Rt. 4, Bright, Ontario N0J 1B0. *Phone:* (519) 684-7309

Contact person: Fred Kurucz

A well-developed farming community which has been going for more than 45 years. This community has also begun several small rural industries. At one point in their history, Community Farm was associated with the Hutterites. In recent years the community has experienced a spiritual renewal and has a particular emphasis on the Christian's relationship to Israel. The present congregation numbers about 100 persons.

Network: Community Farm is associated with Beth-El community in Israel.

Kitchener-Waterloo House Churches

18 Heins Ave., Kitchener, Ontario, N2G 1Z8. *Phone:* (519) 578-4276

Contact person: John W. Miller

There are currently five house churches in the Kitchener-Waterloo House Churches cluster, each with its own unique blend of life together, leadership and outreach. The relationship of the groups and their common life is fostered by a representatives group that meets monthly. Together they sponsor a cycle of three annual retreats, monthly study evenings, bi-weekly Sunday morning worship and family activities. The group began in 1970 and has a special ministry in the area of counseling.

ENGLAND

Brand Hill Baptist Church

53 Kings Way, Oldbury, Worley, West Midland, England B680QD.
Phone: Buringham 021-422-6254
Contact person: John Bedford
   This church of nearly 300 people has been moving into community
after they experienced the charismatic renewal several years ago.
The gifts of the Spirit brought much deep healing through the counseling ministry of their pastor, John Bedford, and others. Out of that
there has developed six extended-family households designed for
ministry and daily fellowship. They are located near a large housing
project in a working class neighborhood.

Community of Celebration

The Thatched House, No. 1 High Street, Wargrave, Berkshire RG10
8JA, England. *Phone:* Wargrave 3327
Contact person: Bob Morris
   This community was established in 1974 and is made up mostly
of English people with some Americans. They have a local focus
to aid and facilitate renewal in parish churches. They have a common
purse and the community is supported primarily by several people
working in various jobs outside of the community.
Network: This fellowship is a member of the Community of Communities, the *usually* parish-centered, fellowship-based circle of communities described in the first chapter of this book.

Darvell (The Bruderhof)

Robertsbridge, Sussex, England TN32 5DR. *Phone:* Robertsbridge
880-626
   A description for the Bruderhof Communities may be found under
the entry for the Woodcrest Community in New York, U.S.A.
Network: The Bruderhof Communities, also known as the Hutterian
Society of Brothers, are part of the Hutterian Church.

London Mennonite House

14, Shepherds Hill, Highgate, London N6 5AQ England. *Phone:* 01-
340-8775
Contact person: Alan Kreider or Robert Zuercher
   This small Christian fellowship began in 1976 as a home for for-
eign students residing in London. It is related with the Mennonite
Board of Missions. Their life together has been rapidly expanding.
Network: They are related to Foyer Grebel in France and Com-
munaute Espagnole Evangelique in Brussels.

Post Green Community

57 Dorchester Road, Lytchett Minster, Poole, Dorset BH16 6JE,
England. *Phone:* Lytchett Minster 2317
Contact person: Gordon Abbott

This community of over 100 people was initially established in 1974 to support the teaching, healing, camp and conference ministry that Thomas Lees and his wife had been led to start six years before. The community operates in a "family life-style" in which each member is treated in a personal way. Sometimes the whole community may have to sacrifice for the sake of one member; sometimes one member may have to sacrifice for the sake of the whole community. But all are called to give of themselves as totally as possible.

Network: This fellowship is a member of the Community of Communities, the *usually* parish-centered, fellowship-based circle of communities described in the first chapter of this book.

The End House

17 Gills Hill Lane, Radlett, Herts WD7 8DE, Great Britain. *Phone:* Radlett 6316

The End House is a branch of the Evangelical Sisterhood of Mary, a fuller description of which can be found under the listing for their community in Germany.

Network: Evangelical Sisterhood of Mary.

FRANCE

Abbaye du Bec Hellouin

F-27800 a Brionne (Eure) France
Contact person: Philibert Zobel

This is one of the oldest Benedictin Abbeys in France. It has been open to the charismatic renewal since 1971 and now has an ecumenical emphasis. There are about 80 people at the Abbey, serving others through hospitality and contemplation.

Centre Missionnaire de Bretagne

Coat-y-Louarn, F-29270 Carhaix, France
Contact person: Yvon Charles

This community which began in 1960 was a very strong supporter of the introduction of the charismatic renewal into France. They share all things in common and have a strong evangelistic and teaching outreach.

Communaute de Bethanie

Chalencon, F-43130 Retournac, France
Contact person: Bernard Jeoffroy

This community of more than 60 members began in 1972 and has a very active ministry among students and with poor people in a Franciscan life-style. However, their evangelization is not denominationally based. They have close ties with groups in Paris and Algeria.

Communaute du Chemin Neuf

49, Montee du Chemin Neuf, F-62300 — Lens, France. *Phone:* (78) 37-88-67
Contact person: Laurent Fabre
This charismatic community of about 150 members began in 1972. They have a strong healing and counseling ministry based in their life together. They publish the French charismatic monthly: *Tychique.*

Communite Chretienne

111, Rue des Stations, F-5900 Lille, France
Contact person: David Berly
This very small community began in 1976 and is devoted primarily to urban evangelism. There are only 15 full members in the community sharing a common life, but their charismatic ministry involves about 300 people.

Communaute de la Nativite

12, Rue Poussin F-87100 Limoges, France. *Phone:* (55) 79-36-96
Contact person: Marie-Th. Agnes
This small group of charismatic believers gathered together in 1975 with a vision of unity between churches. They have been used in a ministry of deliverance and spiritual healing.

Communaute Oecumenique de Taize

Taize 71460 Saint Bengoux, le National, France
This ecumenical monastery of about 80 brothers was founded in the early 1940's and has since been both a model and an inspiration for many other Christian communities in Europe. The community has become additionally well known for the spontaneous Easter celebrations which began a few years ago and now draw tens-of-thousands of tourists, seekers and sincere worshipers each spring.

Communaute La Porte Ouverte

a Lux, F-71100 — Chalon s. Saone, France.
Contact person: Louis Pont
There are about 30 members of this community living in their center in Chalon which began in the early 1960's. About 40 other members are stationed away from the center in mission work. They are one of the principal charismatic, ecumenical centers for the French-speaking European countries.

Communite de la Sainte Croix

F-38450 — St. Barthelemy du Gua, France
Contact person: Jacky Parmentier
This charismatic community of about 20 members began in 1973 and has a powerful ministry of teaching, prayer and praise that involves as many as 200 people. They have some relationship with La Theophanie.

Communaute La Source

27 bis Rue du 14 Juillet, F-62300 — Lens, France
Contact person: Rene Jacob or Jean-Noel Hemar

This charismatic community began in 1975 and shares a burden for unity within the body of Christ. The outreach of the 24 members is primarily evangelization and teaching and they are relating to about 200 people.

Communaute de la Theophanie

B.P. 6070 34 030 — Montpellier Cedex, France. *Phone:* (67) 54 24 05
Contact person: Jacques Langhart

This charismatic Christian community began on Pentecost Monday in 1972 when the initial members covenanted together to seek the Lord in unity of life and prayer, sharing all they had. Following their commitment they experienced the baptism of the Holy Spirit. Today, with about 140 people, they are one of the best-known communities in France and have helped start a network of small fellowships in five other cities. They believe that a submitted body life together is the normal form the church should take as the primary base for evangelism and mission. They enjoy a variety of life situations among their members, both celebates and families, extended households and nuclear family living units. Their primary outreach has been in terms of teaching and renewal in the Spirit within the church.

Foyer Grebel

13, Rue du Val d'Osne, F-94410 Saint Maurice, France *Phone:* 368-38-45
Contact person: Larry Miller

This new and very small fellowship is affiliated with the French Mennonite Mission and the Mennonite Board of Missions. They have a special ministry of hospitality to foreign students in residence in Paris.
Network: They are related to the London Mennonite House and Communaute Espagnole Evangelique in Brussels.

Union de Priere de Charmes

F-07190 — St Sauveur de Montagut, France
Contact person: P. L. Schneider

This long-established group has become an important center of prayer, praise and prophecy. They have been instrumental in helping many other prayer groups start in France.

GERMANY

Christian Residential Group Gut Kuppershof

Kuppershofweg 15, D-5100 Aachen-Richterich, West Germany. *Phone:* 0241/12139 or 13342

Contact person: Klaus Henning

The Kuppershof community came into existence on the initiative of members of an ecumenical community at the university in Aachen at the end of 1972. Today about 21 people are living together as families and single persons, employees as well as students. They are aiming to create a concrete witness to Christ by sharing their lives together.

Evangelical Sisterhood of Mary

P. O. B. 13 01 29, Heidelberger Landstrasse 107, D-6100 Darmstadt 13, West Germany. *Phone:* (06151) 5 10 31

The Sisterhood of Mary was founded in 1947 by Mother Basilea and Mother Martyria as a fulfillment of their conviction that God delights in granting people a "foretaste of heaven" where Jesus Christ has dominion. The miracles of faith that brought about the building of the community as well as the testimony of its members to the importance of total dedication to Jesus with a deep love of a bride for the Bridegroom, and of the value of repentance have moved many people. Mother Basilea Schlink has written many inspirational and devotional items that spring from the life and experience of the Sisterhood.

Network: The Evangelical Sisterhood of Mary has branches in Jerusalem, Greece, England, Italy, Scandinavia, and Arizona, U.S.A.

Gospel Outreach

8 Munchen 82, Barschweg, West Germany. *Phone:* (089) 42-3955
Contact person: Thomas Van Dooren

A fuller description of the Gospel Outreach Ministries can be found under the listing for Eureka, California, U.S.A. This branch in West Germany began in 1975 and has about 65 people involved. There are two households, and the membership is supported by a professional cleaning service and several outside jobs.

Network: Gospel Outreach Ministries.

Integrierte Gemeinde

Herzog Heinrich Straase Nr 18; D-8 Munchen 15 BRD Deutschland, West Germany

This community of about 200 people has a special emphasis on theological research and teaching. They are running two small business operations. About one-third of the people are living together sharing their resources.

Jesus-Bruderschaft Gnadenthal (The Brotherhood of Jesus)

6257 Hunfelden 2, Gnadenthal, West Germany. *Phone:* 06438/2001
648 Belvidere Avenue, Plainfield, New Jersey 07062 U.S.A. *Phone:* (201) 561-0262

The Brotherhood of Jesus is basically a monastic community which began in 1962 and now has about 60 brothers and 60 sisters. The largest group of these people live at their center in Gnadenthal devoted to a life of witness, service and prayer. They have, however, sent out service teams to other locations in Germany, Switzerland, Africa, Israel and the United States. Also there are groups of families associated with the Brotherhood living in other towns in Germany.

Laurentiuskonvent
Laurentiusfoh, D 3549 Wethen, West Germany. *Phone:* 0 56 94-447
Contact person: Paulander Huasmann

This community of about 60 people began in 1959 when three single men decided to live together, sharing what they had, and serving the Lord. Since then they have been joined by other singles and families and have branched out to start a network of groups in other locations in Germany. One major area of their calling is toward realization and sharing the peace which Christ left with the world in John 14:27. The members are permanently convenanted together, seeking the Lord's leading in total community of decision and property. The community is open to every social and educational level, but all members prepare in themselves the freedom to exist among those who are despised and rejected and disinherited, as a constant possibility of brotherly love.

GUATEMALA

Gospel Outreach
Apartado Postal No. 2621, Guatemala City, Central America
Contact person: Jim Degolyer

A fuller description of the Gospel Outreach Ministries can be found under the listing for Eureka, California, U.S.A. This branch in Guatemala City began in 1976 and has about 70 people involved. There are three households, and the membership is supported by funds from the United States since work projects are not currently allowed.
Network: Gospel Outreach Ministries.

ITALY

Agape
Servizio Cristiano, Riesi, Sicily, Italy
Contact person: Tulio Vinay

This community of over 30 members began in 1960 and has a very broad ministry of evangelism, social and economical development to the poor people in their area. Their charismatic life reaches more than 500 people. They have a common industry in knitting and embroidery and in the production of high grade steel gears for industry.

Nomadelfia
C.P. 176, I-58100 Grosseto, Italy

This community of over 50 people began in 1948 and has since been well known for their help and care of abandoned and destitute children. The community is composed of several families living together and sharing a common purse to support their ministry.

LEBANON

People of God

c/o Peter Shebaya, Fine Arts Department, American University of Beirut, P.O. Box 236, Beirut, Lebanon

Contact person: Peter Shebaya

This community had its first beginnings in 1973. Between then and 1975, when the war in Lebanon broke out, they grew in numbers and some of them began living in households. With the outbreak of the war, many were forced by circumstances to come and live with them, and they were drawn into a close and supportive unity. Throughout the fighting the Lord has miraculously protected them from harm and has magnified the light of their witness.

SCOTLAND

Community of Celebration

The Cathedral, Millport, Isle of Cumbrae Scotland KA28 OHE. *Phone:* Millport 738

Contact person: Bill Farra

This community of over 50 people was established in the spring of 1975 by people who came with Graham Pulkingham (some initially from the Church of the Redeemer in Houston, Texas) to set up a base for the International Fisherfolk Team. They see themselves as a servant community to other communities and church leaders in the areas of pastoral and worship life. They are associated with the Scottish Episcopal congregation on their tiny island (population: 900) which is a summer tourist center for the working class residents of Glasgow who flock there by the thousands. The community supports itself through record and tape productions and tourist enterprises in the summer and sends out the traveling ministry team in the winter to aid in the international renewal of the church.

Network: This fellowship is a member of the Community of Communities, the *usually* parish-centered, fellowship-based circle of communities described in the first chapter of this book.

The Iona Community

91 West Princes Street, Glasgow, G4 9BY, Scotland. *Phone:* 041-331 2351

Contact person: Graeme Brown

The Iona Community was founded in 1938 with the intention of enabling the church to relate the Gospel to men in industry who were, and still remain, largely alienated from the organized Church. Six ministers in training and six unemployed craftsmen were brought together to rebuild the Abbey on Iona. Their work together brought much mutual understanding. A resident community now lives at the Abbey and invites others to come and share their life with them. There is a Community House in Glasgow on the mainland which is devoted to peace and discipleship. The community is also experimenting with other living arrangements for its members in households or clusters of homes in different neighborhoods as the center of fellowship and the base for mission. There are 137 members in the community; most of them work in outside jobs.

SWITZERLAND

Communaute de Grandchamps (Protestant Sisters)
CH-3015—Adeuse, Switzerland
This monastery began in the 1950's for single women. Their primary ministry is through contemplation, prayer, hospitality and spiritual retreats.

Jean-Michel et son equipe
Essertines-sur-Yverdon, Suisse, Switzerland
Contact person: Jean-Michel Cravanzola
This charismatic community began in 1972 and now has more than 150 members and a ministry to a much larger group of people. They have been experiencing a very rapid growth recently through a welcome to sinners, a strong evangelism witness and an intensive healing ministry. They are also involved in publishing books and records and have been doing some work with TV.

L'Abri Fellowship
Chalet Les Melezes, 1861 Huemoz, Switzerland
The influence of Francis Schaeffer on modern Christian thought is widespread through his many books, tapes, personal lectures, and especially through the film series "How Should We then Live?" L'Abri is the home of the Schaeffers (Francis and his wife, Edith) and several other people who work with them to keep the chalet open to thousands of guests (usually intellectually oriented students) who come to stay for a short or long period of time seeking the Lord or deepening their Christian faith through study and fellowship.

Appendix B

Reba Place Fellowship

The following material was initially prepared in pamphlet form by Gary Havens. I've included it as an appendix to provide background for this book. Gary and his wife, Jan, were the family Neta and I lived with nine years ago when we were first exploring Christian community. Those early experiences with the Havens are described in *Living Together in a World Falling Apart*. Later the Havens joined Reba Place Fellowship at just about the same time we did—five years ago.

We began in 1957 in one house in Evanston, just north of Chicago, but we trace our roots back through the centuries-old peace church movement to the 16th-century Anabaptists. Their vision is ours: the church as a disciplined brotherhood, determined to obey Jesus Christ, open to all of God's ways, evangelistic by virtue of our shared life of self-sacrificing love.

To acquaint you with who we are we've answered 21 of the questions we hear asked most often.

Do you have to be a Christian before you join the Fellowship?

Bob Shuford (right) answers this question. Bob and his family have been with the Fellowship since 1973. Since then they've increased their family to four children and have helped lead one of the Fellowship's small groups. Bob has also been teaching at National College as an instructor in Social Sciences. Pictured to his left is his wife, Lois.

My first contact with Reba Place Fellowship was as a non-Christian who didn't even want to become a Christian. My wife and I were so moved by the love and peace we felt here—we had been sending our daughter Becky to the Reba Day Nursery which is staffed with Fellowship members—that we were attracted first by that. The spirit of the people here—which I learned later was of the Lord—was so different from anything I had ex-perienced before and so good that I knew then what was the most important thing in my life: to live in that spirit. We were converted by the Lord through this community and became members. I will ever be grateful that the people of Reba Place loved us even when we weren't Christians!

"My Heart trusted in Him, and I am helped ... and with my song will I praise Jehovah ..." So reads a portion of Psalm 28. Led by guitars, violin, cello, piano, and other musical instruments, we sing a wide selection of songs in worship ... some from our traditional Mennonite Hymnals, others from contemporary writers.

How does one become a member?

Since her coming to the Fellowship in 1973, Hope Harley (right) has been a Reba Day Nursery teacher. Before that she worked with missionaries in Peru, South America and as a writer and editor in Wheaton, Illinois. She and her husband, Tom, also a member, were married in 1978.

Before becoming a member, a person usually moves near us and relates to the fellowship as an intentional neighbor. This period (the length of which varies greatly from one individual to another) allows time for coming to understand the basis of our life together and for experiencing that life with us through worship and our daily interactions.

Choosing membership then is a decision to join with us in commitment to a life of open responsiveness to the Lord and to each other.

Are children free not to become members?

Some families have lived in the Fellowship long enough to see their children grow into adulthood. Some of these children have decided to join RPF as adult members. Dave Vogt (left) is one of these second-generation members. Dave's parents brought him with them to the Fellowship in 1963. Since 1974 he has been a member.

As a child growing up at Reba Place I always felt I would be given the freedom as an adult to choose my own lifestyle. Through my teen years, parents and other members encouraged me to make my own autonomous decisions. They communicated the importance of an *adult* commitment, if and when I wanted that.

At one point, community was not for me. But, I still felt supported and even encouraged to investigate life outside Reba Place. When I did become a member, it was without pressure, as my own choice.

How can you accept people telling you what you can or cannot do?

Walt Jones (above) has been a Christian since Easter of 1975. He grew up in New York City and Pennsylvania. Since coming to the Fellowship in 1976 he has worked with the Illinois State Employment Services and for the City of Evanston. Pictured with him are his wife, Elaine, and daughter, Che.

Our life together is based on our covenant relationship with the Lord that we share on a day-to-day basis with our brothers and sisters. One very important portion of this covenant is our obligation to give and receive admonition. This brings us closer to our brothers and sisters, because through this practice we see Christ in one another. In other words, my brothers and sisters do not tell me what I can or can't do; Christ our Lord speaks through them to me.

Our desire is to be in unity, so I am responsible to work toward that unity if there should be any real concern or cause for disappointment.

Formed with patience ... Judy Studenski, a member since 1974, throws a pot on a potter's wheel at her job in Norris University Center at Evanston's Northwestern University.

In your church many of you live together in what are called "households." What is a household and how do you put one together?

Don Lind (left) grew up in Hesston, Kansas and attended Hesston and Goshen (Indiana) Colleges. He and his family (his son, Sam, is pictured on his lap) came to RPF in 1974 along with other folks from the Atlanta (Georgia) Fellowship. He works with D. William Berry and Associates, a Fellowship-staffed business venture.

A household at RPF is a group of people very much put together by the Lord through the guidance of the elders with the affirmation of the whole body of members and especially those who are to be part of the new venture. There is a wide variety of style that gives each one a distinctive personality. Not all households have the same purpose, structure or size. A smaller one might consist of a single family with several singles all sharing a common life. A larger household might consist of several families, single parent families and singles. Life becomes a shared experience with common meals, worship, recreation, buying, work, and so forth.

Household life is an intense experience and calls for careful structures. Mature leadership is necessary, as well as a number of members who can support the household goals and carry out its ministry.

Squeezing together for some fun ... and making good use of a hard-to-see hole, household members pose during a spring outing in a nearby park.

Is a household a good place for a child to grow up?

In 1976 Jim Croegaert (right) brought his family from Lincoln, Illinois where they had been members of the Beth Shalom Fellowship. Since coming to RPF, Jim has worked as Production Coordinator at Niles Township Sheltered Workshop. He and his wife, Janalee (pictured to his left), have three children. Jacob (also pictured) is their youngest.

Children in Fellowship households have not only their own parents to care for them but all of the other adults and older children too. It's like the old-fashioned extended families—where aunts and uncles, grandparents and cousins all took part in the loving care of each child. Of course, with that many people involved it's important to be consistent. Each person must deal with the child according to his or her needs. Shortly after we moved here, our little girl, Anna, began kindergarten. At the end of the first semester she was not doing well. She was having a hard time accepting authority. We were concerned. She had seemed to be an eager learner and had done well in two years of nursery school. Talking about it with the household helped to bring the problem into focus. Before moving here we had lived in a place where she had no friends her own age. Most of her contacts were with young adults. Together with our Reba household we decided to help her relax—to let her be a little girl. She wouldn't have to think of herself as a little adult. Praise God she was relieved of that burden and she's happier now.

To eager listeners ... Richard Friesen reads during an afternoon in nursery school.

You live so closely ...
don't you get into arguments?

Dennis and Maurine Chesley (left) have been in the Fellowship since 1972. They grew up in Jackson, Michigan and Alexandria, Virginia, respectively. They were married two years before coming to Reba Place. Dennis has been supervisor of the Fellowship business office; he and his wife have also been involved in leading a small group.

Yes, we do have conflicts. If it weren't for our commitment to resolve these, we'd probably pack our bags and leave when the going got rough.

But because of our commitment, we believe that conflicts give us the chance to practice our desire to love one another and to give and receive counsel. They force us to evaluate our wrongs, our selfishness and anger. We hope that when we see our sin we will quickly confess it. That gives the best foundation for reconciliation. Jesus's teachings are our guide to resolution: "... go to your brother ..." (Matthew 18).

Praise God that we no longer have to run from conflicts, arguments and hard times.

Even in the cellar ... how good and pleasant it is for brothers to dwell together! In this case, it's "take a morning coffee break together" as the Just Builders, the all-Fellowship work crew relaxes. Guests and visitors often join the crew during their time here.

Do you have any privacy when you live in a large household?

Mary Lipscomb (right) came from Springfield, Missouri, in 1975. Since that time she has worked in our nursery school and with profoundly mentally retarded children in La Paz School in Chicago. She has also worked in several Fellowship households. From her experience of living in two of our largest households, she answers ...

I lived in a household of 24 and found enough privacy. My loft-bed helped. It was a large, carpeted balcony with room for my books and a reading lamp. With my roommate below, it was like a two-story bedroom! More important though is that we are very sensitive to the space we all need for emotional well-being. This means providing enough actual physical space as well as private, quiet time. God knows our needs. When we're listening to Him and to each other, our needs for privacy are met.

Reclaimed furniture ... and home-made bunk-beds help furnish many Fellowship bedrooms, such as this one in a pen and ink illustration by Anne Gavitt, a member of one of the Fellowship's households.

Are you getting too big?

Betty Roddy (left) has seen the Fellowship grow from under 30 members to membership numbering in the hundreds. She has been a member since 1970. Three of her grown children have become members. Pictured with her is her first grandchild, Carl Benjamin Roddy.

It's exciting to grow. After all, our main purpose is to spread the good news and live out together the life we have been given. I find that with the people who have come our life has become richer and more diversified.

It helps to know that when we were thirty members we were afraid that we had grown too big to maintain our sensitivity and support together. But we continued to grow and the Lord showed us how we could be 250 and remain a close-knit church. As long as we're willing to put ourselves in His hands, the life He gives will be here.

We have divided once—to form a rural community in Tiskilwa, Illinois. And we have sister communities in other places—Kansas and Indiana. Within our circle of covenanted community churches we transfer memberships and direct serious inquiries. We try to have no investment either in getting larger or staying as we are.

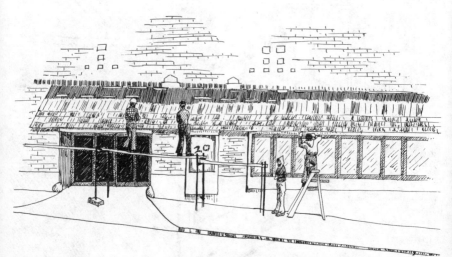

Building together ... from an old warehouse/garage the Fellowship construction crew, Just Builders, made a new meeting house, completed in 1978. Sister communities sent additional help as needed and Fellowship children joined in the work when practical and safe. Here, Fellowship men finish part of the exterior remodeling.

What keeps the Fellowship from becoming ingrown?

Along with his wife Joanna (pictured to his right), John Lehman (above) has been a member of Reba Place since the beginning of the Fellowship. They have three children who have grown up here. John has been a social worker with a number of Chicago-area agencies. In the church he serves as a senior elder.

Jesus is the core of our life. If we lose our first love of Him we are in danger of turning to false gods and self-protection—in danger of being misled or ingrown because we fear some unknown.

In the environment of love that the Lord has given us here, it's natural to want to grow, to learn. To be inquisitive pushes us outward. In the world's maze of knowledge, Jesus, the Word, the Holy Spirit and the Body give us direction and correction.

The constant flow of new people into the Fellowship brings new life and challenge. Our many relationships outside the Fellowship stretch, correct and are a source of counsel. God has richly blessed us!

Caught in a moment of stillness ... two children play in our nursery school. Staffed entirely by members, the school's enrollment includes neighborhood as well as Fellowship children.

Close enough to cramp the pianist's elbows ... Fellowship members, children and guests laugh during a Friday evening skit night, an event usually triggered by a Fellowship couple's announcement of their coming marriage. Small groups and households present songs, skits

and gifts to the couple in celebration of the happy event. Our need for a larger meeting space was met in 1978 with the completion of another meeting house. This provided both a more spacious meeting facility and room for our nursery school to expand their office and play space.

Do elders, the leaders in your church, get more money?

Marv Nisly (right) lived in the Atlanta (Georgia) Fellowship before coming to RPF in 1974. He has two children (his son Philip is pictured with him) and has helped lead one of the households in the Fellowship. Marv also has supervised the Just Builders, the Fellowship work crew.

Actually, in many churches, just the opposite is true: pastors or elders earn *less* than many of the members! Here, elders get as much as other members, but no more. We think that it's important that a member's spiritual position in the church doesn't make any difference either socially or financially.

We believe the Lord has called us to a simple lifestyle. So we own all of our property in common and share our financial resources completely. Those who work at outside jobs (about half of us) turn in their paychecks to the church bookkeeper. Then the church provides for all housing, transportation, phones, food, medical and dental care and a yearly two-week vacation. In addition, we get a monthly allowance to take care of personal needs such as clothing and recreation. Here, a person who earns $30,000 yearly lives on the same level as one who earns $5,000 yearly. This is one way we show our love for one another.

How are elders chosen?

In 1965, Julius Belser (left) came to be part of Reba Place Fellowship, along with his wife Peggy and their three children. Before that he had been pastor of Church of Hope, part of the West Side Christian Parish in Chicago. He and his wife grew up in Elizabethtown, Pennsylvania. Julius works as one of three senior elders here.

Most often elders are chosen because the Lord is already using them in broad service to a number of others ... and we see the fruits. Eldership must be confirmed by the small group who know the individual best. It must also be confirmed by the elders of the Fellowship. The final testing and confirmation is done in the congregational member's meeting. The Biblical passages in Timothy and Titus give guidance, as do the teachings of Jesus regarding the greatest being the servant of all. Finally, when the body comes to unity about the Lord's choice, the prayer for the Spirit's blessing and protection is a joyous experience.

Are women elders in your church?

On his way back to his boyhood home of India, where he had grown up a child of a missionary, and where he himself hoped to serve as a missionary, Virgil Vogt (right) stopped off to visit Reba Place Fellowship, then in its early days. He, along with his wife, Joan, decided to stay. Since that time, he has worked at Chicago State Hospital and as a full-time senior elder.

Currently, one woman serves as an elder. In the past there have been a couple of others. We definitely encourage the women in our community to understand and exercise their leadership gifts. Women have an active part in the total ministry of the Fellowship.

At the same time, we believe God calls husbands to a role of headship in their families. This carries over into the church as well, and right now, the general oversight of the community is given to a group of three men. Normally, we expect men to have overall headship. But we expect them to fulfill this in a humble and Christ-like manner so that the responsible development of leadership gifts in others can have plenty of room for growth.

As David danced before the Lord ... we are learning to express worship and joyfulness to the Lord in praiseful dance. Here, Sara Ewing (left) and Barb Vogt lead a Sunday morning congregation in part of our worship.

I've heard the Fellowship described as a "charismatic" church ... does that mean everyone speaks in tongues or prophesies or shows one of these kinds of gifts?

Hilda Carper (above, second row, third from left) joined Church of Hope in 1959 on Chicago's near-west side. Over the years this church became a sister church to the Fellowship and then joined with us in Evanston in 1966. Hilda grew up in Lancaster County, Pennsylvania and Newport News, Virginia. Since her coming to RPF she has worked as director of Reba Day Nursery and later as a full-time pastor.

Since the Lord is the Giver of the gifts of tongues and prophecy we can receive them joyfully and gratefully. A number of persons in our congregation have the gift of prophecy. Some bring prophetic messages in tongues which are then interpreted. Others prophesy in English. Not everyone—in fact, at this point, only a few persons among us exercise this gift publicly. But it is a gift to all of us when the Lord speaks so personally and directly. How many, or who, exercise a gift is not important. It is important that the Lord has opened channels through which He bestows His gifts upon the Body when and how He wills.

Many of us exercise the gift of tongues for personal worship and petition or in corporate prayer and "free singing." Many do not. It is a means of praising Him beyond words, of letting the Spirit pray through us when we don't know how to pray. It is an aid to growth in our personal relationship with the Lord, but it is not a measure of spirituality.

What is the ministry of the Fellowship?

In 1969, when he has a junior in Evanston Township High School, Matthew Roddy's parents joined RPF. He was born in Northlake, Illinois and attended Goshen College (Indiana) and the University of Illinois at Chicago Circle Campus. In 1973 Matthew (left) became a member. Since then he has been a part of the Just Builders, the Fellowship work crew, managing two apartment buildings housing both Fellowship members and other families.

God does have a ministry for us. I think we need to remind ourselves, though, that our life together is not justified by what we *do;* most important is who we *are:* Christ's Body, God's children, His servants. Out of that understanding we worship and deepen our commitment to His life in loving, accepting and encouraging one another. Through our actions as well as our words we invite others into His kingdom.

We don't have to justify our existence (personally or corporately) by *doing. Being* the sons of God, being the church is most important and actually does more than any "ministry" to advance the Kingdom.

There are by-products—our nursery school, summertime crafts program for all the kids in the neighborhood, the bike repair shop, our involvement in local and national politics, our apartment buildings, our counselling, our planting and oversight of new communities, the network of church communities we belong to, our denominational missionary efforts. But these are affirmations and by-products, not justifications.

Preparing to sail on Lake Michigan ... Russ Harris adjusts the main sheet on the "Nina B", a boat reclaimed from the salvage yard, repaired and refitted entirely by Fellowship workers ... some of them children.

What are your beliefs?

Allan Howe (left) and his wife, Jeanne, came to Reba Place via Church of Hope in Chicago in 1969. They were married in 1965 and have three children. While they've been in the Fellowship, they've been involved in one of the earliest households and Allan has studied for his Ph.D. in New Testament at Garrett/Northwestern University.

As Christians we start with Jesus. For us He is Lord and Saviour, Son of God and man among men, teacher of truth and healer of the nations. He came as Israel's promised Messiah, suffered and died confronting human sin with the love of God, and rose from death by God's power. He now reigns in heaven until He returns with God's full justice. His rule is visible on earth in the Spirit-filled life of His people, the Church.

We believe that the Lord is present in our midst, speaking to us and guiding us in a lively, daily way as we listen and yield. That is our basis for discernment, authority and ministry.

We believe that God desires all persons to discover their identity as His children. All who turn from their sin and reach out to their waiting heavenly Father find themselves within a new family gathered around Jesus.

We see the distinctive convictions and practices of that family reflected quite clearly in the witness of the sixteenth-century Anabaptists. Like them we view God's church family as a community of believers baptized only upon individual confession of faith. Like them we hold Jesus' way and words to reveal truly God's direction for His people: unreserved love and sharing, honesty and mutual responsibility in relationships, the renunciation of coercion and violence, active outreach to the world in service and witness. Like the Anabaptists we believe that such living is possible only by the grace of God and the power of His Spirit. He enables, we follow, and what begins with faith in the Lord Jesus leads to growing experience with Him.

Why did you join a denomination?

Born a child of Russian Jewish parents in a suburb of Warsaw, Poland, Vera Stoehr (left) came to the Fellowship in 1970, via Jerusalem. Since her time here she has lived in one of our first-formed households. She is a librarian at the University of Chicago.

In 1976 we asked to become a part of the Mennonite Church as well as the Brethren Church. This was our way of acknowledging our debt and commitment to the Anabaptist vision and a way to identify ourselves with those who have the same vision. We also wanted to take part in Kingdom activities that are beyond the capacity of individual congregations, such as the Mennonite Central Committee, Brethren Volunteer Service, missionary outreach, Christian education publications, etc. We also wanted to be able to give and receive admonition as a congregation.

Most of us do not come from Mennonite or Brethren backgrounds, but came to the Fellowship because we were attracted to the Kingdom of God ways which these denominations have taken seriously: pacifism, the believers' church, social concern, simplicity, community, humility.

For me personally it's a special experience: I who am ethnically Jewish, together with my brothers and sisters here, have become the new Israel; and I, who am not ethnically Mennonite or Brethren, now hold the Anabaptist vision as my heritage! I thank the Lord for it.

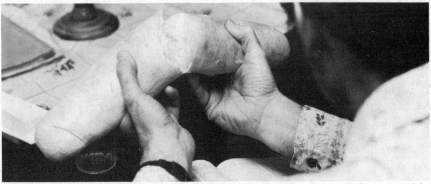

Jesus broken for us ... symbolized by His blessed bread. He is the focal point of our entire life, all our efforts, our pleasures, our prayers and hopes for our children. Those who join us join more than a community ... they join a church.

Who gets counselling at Reba Place?

Russ Harris (left) came in 1971 from Lansing, Michigan, where he taught at Michigan State University. Since coming, he has been an assistant professor at Oakton Community College and a full-time elder for the church.

In one sense, everyone receives counselling. Picture a wide range of types of counselling:

On one end of the range is a simple sharing of a person's walk with the Lord. Has he experienced the forgiveness of his sins? Has he accepted Christ's sacrifice for them on the cross? As a person deeply confesses his specific sins and his general self-centered orientation he sees that his helplessness and drive to survive are barriers which keep him from receiving the love and peace he's been searching for.

Awareness of this is with each of us daily as we share our present struggles and growth and respond to the new challenges the Lord gives us. In this sense, everyone at Reba Place receives counsel.

On the other end of the range, though, is the deeper therapy for those who have experienced a traumatic crisis or deprivation. As these folks are ready and as the Lord leads we try to walk back through these difficult experiences with them and with the Lord. By ourselves, we're powerless; but the Lord seems to know what they need. We praise God for the blessings which He gives through these various counselling relationships.

Trees, grass and concrete ... as an urban church/community we've learned to use our limited space fully. Fences keep recreational areas clean and small children safely away from cars and work areas. Fellowship families usually take a non-urban vacation each year.

Do you have your own school?

Jerry Lind (right) and his wife, Marcia, who are parents of three school-age children, came in 1971 from Sarasota, Florida. They both studied at Goshen College in Indiana. For three years, Jerry taught in an Evanston grade school. He's also worked as a counsellor in the Alcohol Outpatient Program in the Community Hospital of Evanston.

We operate a nursery school for Fellowship families as well as others. As a day care center we've been able to invite lower income families to join in the program. We're grateful that God has provided an arrangement which serves the needs of neighborhood families and gives our own young children a secure place to learn and play with other children.

Our school-age children attend the Evanston schools. They provide quality education and have been responsive and accepting. Our children do encounter behavior and values that run counter to Fellowship life, but they have a strong Fellowship identity and feel the support of other Fellowship children. Though there are occasional problems, using the public schools does provide a manageable exposure to other ways of life through which we have been able to help our children understand and integrate more deeply what is distinctive and valuable about the Kingdom way of life.

Neighborhood children weave ... in our summer crafts program staffed by members of the Fellowship and summer volunteer workers. In a large, cool basement room, Fellowship children as well as others join in activities that include over a hundred children each year.

How do people get married in the Fellowship?

Nevin and Judy Belser (right) were married July 2, 1977. Nevin grew up in Church of Hope in Chicago where his father, Julius, was pastor, and in the Fellowship; Judy came from Sarasota, Florida and New Hampshire, where she was born. Since their time here, they've been students and Nevin has worked as a Salvation Army Emergency Case Aid Worker.

When we discovered our special feelings for one another, the first step was for both of us to talk to our pastors. They helped us to ask ourselves if we were ready for this once-in-a-lifetime decision. Then we began the process of our courtship. It got careful attention and guidance from the entire church body. At each step they gave their support and discernment. We were especially careful not to let the physical aspect of our relationship get ahead of the rest of it. Having that kind of relationship in the Fellowship is *fun* as well as real *work*. We had problems, but we worked on them. We didn't ignore them and hope they'd go away after we got married. We continually grew in knowledge of each other. It's a wonderful, rich feeling to get married knowing that it's right and you're ready and you'll have all the love and support you'll need in the people around you in future years.

Something old, something new ... members of the L'Hayim small group prepare an apartment for a soon-to-be-wedded couple—hoping to transform something old into something new, fresh and enjoyable. Mark Steinbrecker (left), Matthew Roddy (center) and Barb Vogt (right) join in the work in a Fellowship apartment building.

Do you believe this is the best way to live?

Just before they moved here, Roger and Alice Golden (left) lived and worked with migrant workers in Immokalee, Florida. Roger grew up in northern Indiana and Alice in Iowa. They have three children.

Alice answers first ...

For me the best way to live is to love the Lord and to know His love. That's most important and it's what makes any way best. The close contact, the type of caring that this living situation brings have been *extremely* important to me. The Lord has used the life here to draw me to Himself, to heal my marriage, to enrich me as a parent. So for me it has been very good. God has used it—and it has been His best for me.

Roger continues ...

It has been the best for me because the Lord has called me here to live out my life in a deeply committed body. This has been the setting where the Lord could work with me and bring my life under His control. I have needed structure and authority and have found it. For others the particular Reba Place form may not be the way. Each person needs to seek God's plan for accountability, interdependence and submission for his life. This may lead to a church/community such as Reba Place, or it may lead to other congregations where the core of their life is a deep commitment to each other in the Body of Christ.

Unless the Lord build the house ...
The Just Builders near completion of a new roof on one of the Fellowship houses.

Reba Place Fellowship is part of a larger network of church communities with whom we are covenanted together in formal commitment. These include:

Fellowship of Hope
326 Cleveland
Elkhart, Indiana 46514

Plow Creek Fellowship
Tiskilwa, Illinois 61368

New Creation Fellowship
417 West 11th
Newton, Kansas 67114

Your inquiries regarding these communities are welcome.